COOL HOTELS

ASIA/PACIFIC

edited by Martin Nicholas Kunz

teNeues

Melbourne

Auckland

Sydney

Queenstown

Yangon

Bangkok

Chiang Mai

Singapore

Phnom Penh

Hanoi

Jakarta

Beijing

Udaipur

Hong Kong

Mumbai

Bali

Jaipur

Shanghai

Mochi

Delhi

Sun Moon Lake

Nasu Gun

Uttaranchal

Taipei

Tokyo

Cool Hotels

ASIA/PACIFIC

Luxury
between Orient and Occident

The door to paradise is wide open. A porter rushes by carrying the luggage and hands over the room key. One looks around the room expectantly, discovers fragrant jasmine blossoms in the vase, fresh pineapple in the fruit basket, a fluffy bathrobe on the bed, and with a pounding heart dares to take a first look out the window or from the balcony. A dream vista. Bliss. One has arrived. What do we find fascinating in the five-star world where the personnel or even a personal butler anticipates one's every wish? It is the feeling of being one of the chosen few. One is—fascinated by the intensity with which one is looked after—worth more than in daily life, seemingly light-years away. It flatters the ego-being courted, groomed, pampered.

It is exactly Asia where luxury is newly defined. In the pulsing mega-cities such as Bangkok, in the deserts of Rajasthan, on the slopes of the Himalaya, and in Balinese rain forests, luxury hotels are opening their gates—and courting the guests with novel offers: first-rate high-tech is an offering of the new Intercontinental Marine Drive in Mumbai where one can watch the newest Bollywood films from bed and from the bathtub on a swivel plasma television. In the Devi Garh Palace near Udaipur, Ayurveda doctors or astrologists can be consulted, and ecologically oriented resorts like the Four Seasons Bali at Sayan are committed to letting one experience nature.

Regardless of what kind of hotel is involved, they all satisfy the needs of stressed-out working persons from the western world: on the one hand, letting go of the daily routine for a moment, on the other, filling the senses with unusual perceptions. Luxurious components such as stylish interiors in gentle color combinations impart a feeling of peace, letting us glide into another world—as in The Lalu on the magical Sun Moon Lake in Taiwan created by the Australian architectural office of Kerry Hill Architects. Or in Sukhothai in Bangkok, furnished by the interior designer Ed Tuttle. Culinary delicacies also revive the senses, Thai massages promote body awareness, seclusion helps one reflect. Luxury hotels are total works of art that have good taste.

Two kinds of hotels especially highlight new trends in Asia and Oceania: nostalgia and nature. The nostalgic hotels already existed when today's travelers couldn't even walk, such as the majestic Taj Mahal Palace & Tower in Mumbai from 1903, the Sofitel Metropole in Hanoi from 1901 and the Oriental in Bangkok and a Maharaja's fortress palace near Udaipur. These hotels steeped in history create access into earlier worlds. Some palaces are so authentically spruced up one believes one can still see the pomp of old days in the suites, in the overall impression of an old butler. Reliving history is staged as in the Rajvilas in Jaipur where adventurers can overnight in tents just as Indian regents used to on trips. These hotels hand down the history and traditions of a country in a beautiful way. Even today, they appear as kingly mansions, surrounded by a secretive aura to which the average citizen has no access.

On the other hand, hotels in touch with nature lure: they present their guests the Garden of Eden in which an archaic timescale is present. Resorts such as the Four Seasons in Chiang Mai in Thailand or its sister resort in Bali or the neighboring first house of the Aman resort Amandari in the midst of rice terraces equal botanic paradises. The guest contributes to the protection of flora and fauna simply by being there. The environment and indigenous people then benefit from the price for this paradise. The world is more gently discovered here.

This magnificent volume, with inviting photographs, picks up on these trends and presents the most beautiful luxury hotels in Asia, Australia, and New Zealand.

Camilla Péus

Luxus zwischen Ost und West

Die Tür zum Paradies steht weit offen. Ein Portier eilt herbei, trägt die Koffer und übergibt die Zimmerschlüssel. Erwartungsvoll schaut man sich im Zimmer um, entdeckt duftende Jasminblüten in der Vase, frische Ananas im Obstkorb, einen flauschigen Bademantel auf dem Bett und wagt mit klopfendem Herzen den ersten Blick aus dem Fenster oder vom Balkon. Traumaussicht. Glücksgefühle. Man ist angekommen. Was fasziniert uns an der Fünf-Sterne-Welt, wo einem das Personal oder gar ein persönlicher Butler jeden Wunsch von den Augen abliest? Es ist das Gefühl, auserwählt zu sein. Man ist – fasziniert von der Intensität, mit der man umsorgt wird – mehr Wert als im Alltag, der Lichtjahre entfernt scheint. Es schmeichelt dem Ego, hofiert, gepflegt und verwöhnt zu werden.

Gerade in Asien wird Luxus neu definiert. In pulsierenden Mega-Städten wie Bangkok, in den Wüsten Rajasthans, auf den Hängen des Himalaja und im balinesischen Regenwald öffnen Luxushotels ihre Tore – und buhlen mit neuartigen Angeboten um die Gäste: Hightech der Extraklasse bietet das neue Intercontinental Marine Drive in Mumbai, wo man auf schwenkbaren Plasma-Fernsehern neueste Bollywood-Filme vom Bett und von der Badewanne aus sehen kann. Im Palast Devi Garh bei Udaipur können Ayurveda-Ärzte oder Astrologen konsultiert werden, und ökologisch orientierte Resorts wie das Four Seasons Bali at Sayan haben sich das Erleben von Natur auf die Fahnen geschrieben.

Ganz gleich um welchen Hoteltyp es sich handelt, sie alle befriedigen ein Bedürfnis gestresster Berufstätiger der westlichen Welt: Einerseits, einen Augenblick den Alltag loszulassen, andererseits, die Sinne mit außergewöhnlichen Wahrnehmungen zu füllen. Luxus-Komponenten wie stilvolle Interieurs in sanften Farbnuancen vermitteln eine atmosphärische Ruhe, die uns hinübergleiten lässt in eine andere Welt – so wie im The Lalu am magischen Sun Moon Lake in Taiwan, das von dem australischen Architekturbüro Kerry Hill Architects geschaffen wurde. Oder im Sukhothai in Bangkok, das Interieurdesigner Ed Tuttle ausstattete. Auch kulinarische Genüsse beleben die Sinne, Thai-Massagen fördern das Körperbewusstsein, Abgeschiedenheit hilft, sich zu besinnen. Luxushotels sind Gesamtkunstwerke des guten Geschmacks.

Zwei Arten von Hotels markieren besonders in Asien und Ozeanien neue Trends: Nostalgie und Natur. Die nostalgischen Hotels gab es schon, als der Reisende von heute noch nicht einmal laufen konnte, wie das majestätische Taj Mahal Palace & Tower in Mumbai von 1903, das Sofitel Metropole in Hanoi von 1901 oder das Oriental in Bangkok und der Festungspalast eines Maharajas bei Udaipur. Diese geschichtsträchtigen Häuser schaffen Zugänge in frühere Welten. Man glaubt den Glanz vergangener Tage noch in den Suiten zu sehen, im Gesichtsausdruck eines alten Butlers, so authentisch ist mancher Palast hergerichtet. Das Nacherleben von Geschichte wird inszeniert, wie in den Rajvilas in Jaipur, wo Abenteuerlustige in fürstlichen Zelten übernachten können, wie es indische Regenten auf Reisen taten. Es sind Hotels, die auf schöne Weise Geschichte und Tradition des Landes überliefern. Noch heute erscheinen sie wie Königshäuser, umgeben von einer geheimnisvollen Aura, zu denen Normalbürger keinen Zugang haben.

Andererseits locken Hotels mit Naturverbundenheit: Sie präsentieren ihren Gästen den Garten Eden, in dem ein archaisches Zeitmaß gilt. Resorts wie das Four Seasons in Chiang Mai in Thailand oder sein Schwester-Resort in Bali bzw. das benachbarte erste Haus der Amanresorts Amandari inmitten von Reisterrassen gleichen botanischen Paradiesen. Der Gast trägt durch seine bloße Anwesenheit zum Schutz von Flora und Fauna bei. Der Preis für das Paradies kommt dabei auch der Umwelt und der einheimischen Bevölkerung zu Gute. Die Welt wird hier sanfter entdeckt.

Dieser prächtige, mit einladenden Fotos bebilderte Band greift diese Trends auf und präsentiert die schönsten Luxushotels in Asien, Australien und Neuseeland.

Camilla Péus

Le luxe
entre l'Orient et l'Occident

La porte du paradis vous est grande ouverte. Un portier accourt à votre rencontre, porte les valises et vous remet les clés de la chambre. Plein d'attente, on jette un coup d'œil dans la chambre, on découvre des fleurs de jasmin à l'agréable parfum dans le vase, des ananas frais dans la corbeille de fruits, un peignoir moelleux sur le lit et on ose, le cœur battant, jeter un premier regard dehors, de la fenêtre ou du balcon. Une vue de rêve. Sensations de bonheur. On est arrivé. Qu'est-ce qui nous fascine dans le monde des cinq étoiles où le personnel, ou même un maître d'hôtel lit vos souhaits dans vos yeux ? C'est le sentiment d'être l'élu. On a – fasciné par l'intensité avec laquelle on s'occupe de nous – plus de valeur qu'au quotidien, qui semble se trouver à des années lumières de nous. Etre courtisé, soigné et dorloté flatte l'ego.

C'est justement en Asie que le luxe trouve une nouvelle définition. Dans les villes géantes et bouillonnantes comme Bangkok, dans les déserts du Rajasthand, sur les versants de l'Himalaya et dans la forêt tropicale balinaise, les hôtels de luxe ouvrent leurs portes – et séduisent leurs hôtes avec des offres nouvelles : le nouveau Marine Drive à Mumbai offre de la haute technologie de première classe, on peut y regarder du lit et de la baignoire les films Bollywood les plus récents sur des téléviseurs plasma pivotants. Au palais Devi Garh, près de Udaipur, vous pouvez consulter des médecins Ayurveda ou des astrologues, et des hôtels de tourisme mettant l'accent sur l'écologie comme le Four Seasons Bali à Sayan se sont fixés comme objectif l'expérience de la nature.

Quel que soit le type d'hôtel dont il s'agit, ils satisfont tous un besoin des personnes actives et stressées du monde occidental : d'un côté, lâcher le quotidien pendant un instant, d'un autre côté, remplir les sens de perceptions extraordinaires. Les composantes du luxe comme les intérieurs de bon goût dans de douces nuances colorées procurent une atmosphère de calme qui nous fait glisser dans un autre monde – comme dans The Lalu au Sun Moon Lake magique à Taiwan qui a été créé par le bureau australien Kerry Hill Architects. Ou dans le Sukhothai à Bangkok qui a été aménagé par le designer d'intérieur Ed Tuttle. Les plaisirs culinaires éveillent également les sens, les massages Thaï favorisent la prise de conscience de son corps, l'isolement aide à réfléchir. Les hôtels de luxe sont des œuvres d'art totales et qui ont du style.

Deux types d'hôtels marquent des nouvelles tendances particulièrement en Asie et en Océanie : la nostalgie et la nature. Il y avait déjà les hôtels nostalgiques lorsque le touriste d'aujourd'hui ne savait pas encore marcher, comme le majestueux Taj Mahal Palace & Tower de 1903, le Sofitel Metropole à Hanoi de 1901 ou l'Oriental à Bangkok et le palais forteresse d'un Maharadjah près d'Udaipur. Ces maisons porteuses d'histoire créent des accès aux mondes qui ont précédé. On croit encore voir la splendeur des jours passés dans les suites, dans l'expression sur le visage d'un ancien maître d'hôtel, certains palais sont aménagés de manière si authentique. Le partage de l'histoire est mis en scène, comme dans les Rajvilas à Jaipur, où les hôtes à l'âme aventurière pourront passer une nuit dans des tentes princières comme le faisaient les souverains indiens en voyage. Ce sont des hôtels qui transmettent d'une belle manière l'histoire et la tradition du pays. Aujourd'hui encore, ils semblent être des maisons royales, entourés d'une aura mystérieuse, et auxquels les citoyens normaux n'ont pas accès.

D'un autre côté, ce sont les hôtels proches de la nature qui attirent : ils présentent à leurs hôtes le jardin d'Eden dans lequel s'applique une mesure du temps archaïque. Des hôtels de tourisme tel le Four Seasons à Chiang Mai en Thaïlande ou son hôtel de tourisme sœur à Bali, voire la première maison voisine des hôtels de tourisme Aman Amandari au milieu des terrasses de riz ressemblent à des paradis botaniques. Le client contribue à la protection de la flore et de la faune par sa simple présence. Le prix pour le paradis bénéficie ainsi également à l'environnement et à la population locale. On découvre ici le monde de façon plus douce.

Ce superbe ouvrage, illustré de photos invitant au voyage, reprend ces tendances et présente les plus beaux hôtels de luxe en Asie, en Australie et en Nouvelle-Zélande.

Camilla Péus

Lujo entre Oriente y Occidente

La puerta al paraíso está abierta de par en par. Un portero acude deprisa, lleva las maletas y entrega la llave de la habitación. Llenos de ilusión damos una vuelta por la habitación, descubrimos jazmines perfumados en el florero, piña fresca en el cesto de las frutas, un suave albornoz sobre la cama y, con el corazón palpitante, nos arriesgamos a dar el primer vistazo desde la ventana o desde el balcón. Una vista de ensueño. Sensación de felicidad. Hemos llegado. ¿Qué es lo que nos fascina del mundo de cinco estrellas, donde el personal o incluso un mayordomo personal nos satisface todos los deseos? Es la sensación de sentirse único. Fascinados por la intensidad con que se nos llena de atenciones, nos sentimos más valiosos que en la vida diaria que parece estar a años luz de distancia. Nos alimenta el ego que nos sirvan, nos cuiden y nos mimen.

Especialmente en Asia el lujo adquiere un nuevo significado. En las vibrantes metrópolis como Bangkok, en los desiertos de Rajastán, en las pendientes del Himalaya y en las selvas tropicales de Bali abren sus puertas los hoteles de lujo —y compiten por los clientes con innovadoras ofertas: Alta tecnología de primerísima calidad se ofrece en el nuevo Intercontinental Marine Drive de Mumbai, donde uno puede ver las últimas películas de Bollywood desde la cama o desde la bañera en un televisor plasma giratorio. En el Palast Devi Garh de Udaipur se puede consultar con los médicos Ayurveda o con los astrólogos, y centros turísticos de inclinación ecológica, como el Four Seasons Bali en Sayan, tienen como objetivo vivir la naturaleza.

No importa de qué tipo de hotel se trata, todos satisfacen las necesidades del profesional estresado del mundo occidental: Por un lado, romper por un instante con la rutina diaria, por otro, colmar los sentidos con percepciones extraordinarias. Los componentes de lujo, tales como elegantes espacios interiores en delicados tonos, proporcionan un ambiente de paz que nos transporta a otro mundo —como sucede en The Lalu, en el mágico Sun Moon Lake de Taiwan, construido por la oficina de arquitectura australiana Kerry Hill Architects. O en el Sukhothai de Bangkok, decorado por el diseñador de interiores Ed Tuttle. También los placeres culinarios estimulan los sentidos, los masajes thai ayudan a que tengamos conciencia de nuestro cuerpo, el aislamiento propicia la reflexión. Los hoteles de lujo son completas obras de arte del buen gusto.

Dos clases de hoteles imponen la moda, especialmente en Asia y Oceanía: Los nostálgicos y aquellos enfocados en la naturaleza. Los primeros ya existían cuando el viajero de hoy andaba en pañales, como el majestuoso Taj Mahal Palace & Tower in Mumbai, de 1903, el Sofitel Metropole de Hanoi, de 1901, o el Oriental de Bangkok y el palacio de un Maharajá en Udaipur. Estas construcciones cargadas de historia abren la entrada a mundos anteriores. Uno cree ver el esplendor del pasado en las suites, en el rostro de un viejo mayordomo, así de auténticos son algunos de estos palacios. Vivir de nuevo la historia es posible, por ejemplo, en el Rajvilas en Jaipur, donde el viajero aventurero puede dormir en tiendas de campaña principescas, como antaño hicieran los soberanos indios cuando iban de viaje, de manera hermosa transmiten la historia y la tradición de un país. Todavía hoy parecen casas reales rodeadas de un aura misteriosa, a las cuales el ciudadano común y corriente no tiene acceso.

Por otro lado, los hoteles ligados a la naturaleza también seducen: Éstos le ofrecen a sus huéspedes el Edén, donde rige una concepción arcaica del tiempo. Resorts como el Four Seasons de Chiang Mai en Tailandia o su resort gemelo en Bali o bien el primero de los Aman resorts, el Amandari, en medio de terrazas de arroz, semejan paraísos botánicos. El huésped contribuye con su mera presencia a la protección de la flora y la fauna. El precio por el paraíso también beneficia al medio ambiente y a la población local. Aquí se descubre suavemente el mundo.

Este volumen maravilloso, ilustrado con seductoras fotografías, captura estas tendencias y presenta los hoteles de lujo más hermosos de Asia, Australia y Nueva Zelanda.

Camilla Péus

Il lusso tra l'Est e l'Ovest

Si spalanca la porta del paradiso. Un portiere accorre, porta i bagagli e consegna le chiavi della camera. Ci si guarda intorno pieni di aspettativa: nel vaso si scoprono fiori di gelsomino profumati, nel cesto della frutta ananas freschi, sul letto un accappatoio morbido, e col cuore palpitante si azzarda il primo sguardo dalla finestra o dal balcone. Vista da sogno. Sensazioni di felicità. Si è arrivati. Che cosa ci affascina del mondo a cinque stelle, dove il personale o addirittura un butler personale sa leggere negli occhi ogni desiderio? È la sensazione di appartenere agli eletti. Si ha l'impressione – affascinati dall'intensità delle cure con cui si viene assistiti – di avere più valore che nella vita quotidiana, lontana ormai anni luce. Lusinga l'ego essere circondati di gentilezze e premure, venire viziati.

Il lusso trova proprio in Asia una nuova definizione. Nelle megalopoli pulsanti come Bangkok, nei deserti del Rajasthan, sulle pendici dell'Himalaja e nella foresta pluviale di Bali gli hotel di lusso aprono le porte – e con nuove proposte si ingraziano gli ospiti: high tech fuoriclasse viene offerto dal nuovo Intercontinental Marine Drive, dove su televisori al plasma orientabili si possono vedere dal letto o dalla vasca da bagno gli ultimi film di Bollywood. Nel palazzo di Devi Garh presso Udaipur si possono consultare medici ayurvedici o astrologi, mentre resort di indirizzo ecologico come il Four Seasons di Bali at Sayan hanno fatto della vita nella natura la loro bandiera.

Poco importa di quale tipo di hotel si tratti, tutti quanti soddisfanno un'esigenza degli occidentali stressati dal lavoro: da una parte mollare per un attimo la vita quotidiana, dall'altra inondare i sensi di percezioni straordinarie. Componenti del lusso come gli interni di classe in tenui sfumature cromatiche diffondono un'atmosfera tranquilla, che ci fa scivolare in un altro mondo – così al The Lalu sul magico Sun Moon Lake a Taiwan, creato dallo studio di architettura australiano Kerry Hill Architects. Oppure al Sukhothai di Bangkok, arredato dal designer di interni Ed Tuttle. Anche i piaceri della tavola vivificano i sensi, i massaggi tailandesi favoriscono la consapevolezza fisica, l'isolamento aiuta a riflettere. Gli hotel di lusso sono capolavori complessivi del buon gusto.

Due tipi di hotel tracciano, particolarmente in Asia e in Oceania, nuovi trend: nostalgia e natura. Gli hotel della nostalgia c'erano già quando il viaggiatore di oggi non sapeva nemmeno camminare, come il maestoso Taj Mahal Palace & Tower di Mubai del 1903, il Sofitel Metropole di Hanoi del 1901, l'Oriental di Bangkok o il palazzo-fortezza di un maragià presso Udaipur. Questi edifici carichi di storia danno l'accesso a mondi che furono. Si crede di vedere ancora lo splendore del passato nelle suite, nell'espressione del volto di un vecchio butler, così autentiche appaiono alcune sistemazioni di antichi palazzi. Viene messa in scena la storia per riviverla, come nel Rajvilas di Jaipur, dove gli amanti dell'avventura possono dormire in tende principesche, proprio come facevano i regnanti indiani quando erano in viaggio. Sono hotel che in un modo bello trasmettono storie e tradizioni del paese. Ancora oggi appaiono come regge avvolte in un'aura misteriosa, alle quali i normali cittadini non hanno accesso.

Gli hotel legati alla natura attirano altrimenti: presentano ai loro ospiti il giardino dell'Eden, in cui vige una scansione del tempo arcaica. Resort come il Four Seasons di Chiang Mai o il suo omologo di Bali, oppure la vicina Amandari, la prima casa di Amanresort, in mezzo a terrazze di riso sono veri e propri paradisi botanici. L'ospite, con la sua sola presenza, contribuisce alla difesa della flora e della fauna. Il prezzo per il paradiso torna nello stesso tempo a beneficio anche dell'ambiente e della popolazione locale. Qui il mondo viene scoperto con discrezione.

Questo splendido volume, illustrato con invitanti foto riprende i trend in voga, e presenta i più belli e lussuosi hotel in Asia, in Australia e in Nuova Zelanda.

Camilla Péus

The Imperial
New Delhi, India

King palms tower into the sky over the white hotel walls emphasize the vertical architecture of the grand Art Deco building. The historic hotel was built in 1931 by Bromfield, one of Sir Edwin Lutyens' associates. It greets its guests in a gold leaf ornamented atrium in the midst of Delhi's shopping and commercial district. The hotel collection's antiques, crystal chandeliers and works of art decorate the rooms and halls. The city-oasis shady veranda offers the perfect set for an English five o'clock tea.

Königspalmen ragen vor den weißen Mauern des Hotels in den Himmel und betonen die vertikale Architektur des grandiosen Art déco-Baus. Das traditionsreiche Hotel, das der Architekt Bromfield, einer der Partner von Sir Edwin Lutyens, 1931 erbaute, empfängt seine Gäste im blattgoldverzierten Atrium mitten im Einkaufs- und Geschäftsviertel Delhis. Antiquitäten, Kristallleuchter und Kunstwerke aus der Sammlung des Hotels dekorieren Zimmer und Flure. Die perfekte Kulisse für einen englischen Five o'clock tea bietet die schattige Veranda der Großstadt-Oase.

Les palmiers royaux s'élèvent dans le ciel devant les murs blancs de l'hôtel et soulignent l'architecture verticale du splendide bâtiment en art déco. L'hôtel riche en traditions, réalisé par l'architecte Bromfield, un associé de Sir Edwin Lutyens en 1931, reçoit ses hôtes dans un atrium décoré de feuilles d'or en plein centre du quartier commerçant et du quartier des affaires de Delhi. Les antiquités, les lustres en cristal et les œuvres d'art de la collection de l'hôtel décorent les chambres et les couloirs. La véranda ombragée de l'oasis de la grande ville offre la coulisse parfaite pour un thé anglais à cinq heures.

Palmas reales se elevan hacia el cielo delante de los muros blancos del hotel y acentúan la arquitectura vertical de la grandiosa construcción Art Deco. Este hotel de larga tradición, construido por el arquitecto Bromfield, uno de los asociados de Sir Edwin Lutyens, en 1931, recibe a sus huéspedes en el atrio decorado con oro batido en medio de la zona comercial de Nueva Delhi. Las habitaciones y los pasillos están decorados con antigüedades, arañas de cristal y obras de arte pertenecientes a la colección del hotel. El escenario perfecto para el te inglés de las cinco de la tarde lo ofrece el porche sombreado de este oasis de la gran ciudad.

Palme regali si innalzano verso il cielo davanti alle mura bianche dell'hotel e sottolineano l'architettura verticale del grandioso edificio art déco. Lo storico hotel, eretto nel 1931 dall'architetto Bromfield, un collegare di sir Edwin Lutyens, nel centro del quartiere dello shopping e degli affari di Delhi, accoglie i suoi ospiti nell'atrio decorato in oro. Oggetti d'antiquariato, lampadari di cristallo e opere d'arte della collezione dell'hotel abbelliscono camere e corridoi. Lo sfondo perfetto per un five o'clock tea all'inglese viene offerto dall'ombrosa veranda nell'oasi della grande città.

The 234 spacious rooms and suites are comfortable shelters in the center of Delhi.

Die 234 geräumigen Zimmer und Suiten sind komfortable Zufluchten im Zentrum Delhis.

Les 234 chambres et suites spacieuses sont des refuges confortables au centre de Delhi.

Las 234 amplias habitaciones y suites son un refugio confortable en el centro de Nueva Dehli.

Le 260 ampie camere e suite sono rifugi confortevoli nel centro di Dehli.

Gleaming marble floors, noble chandeliers, and antique paintings are waiting for the guests. The sandstone sculptures in the patio of the Asian specialties restaurant are especially impressive.

Schimmernde Marmorböden, edle Kronleuchter und antike Gemälde erwarten die Gäste. Besonders eindrucksvoll sind die Sandsteinskulpturen im Patio des asiatischen Spezialitätenrestaurants.

Des sols de marbre brillants, des lustres splendides et des peintures antiques attendent les hôtes. Les sculptures en grès dans le patio du restaurant de spécialités asiatiques sont particulièrement impressionnantes.

Suelos de mármol relucientes, arañas preciosas y cuadros antiguos esperan a los huéspedes. Especialmente impresionantes son las esculturas de arenisca que se encuentran en el patio del restaurante que ofrece especialidades asiáticas.

Pavimenti di marmo luccicanti, preziosi lampadari a corona e pitture antiche attendono gli ospiti. Particolarmente notevoli sono le sculture di pietra arenaria nel ristorante di cucina tipica asiatica.

East meets west: *in the Spice Route restaurant, one sits under carvings and paintings that are fit to be in a museum. Gourmets have a choice among four restaurants, two bars, and the charming Atrium.*

East meets West: *Im Restaurant Spice Route sitzt man unter museumsreifen Schnitzarbeiten und Gemälden. Feinschmecker haben die Wahl zwischen vier Restaurants, zwei Bars und dem Atrium.*

East meets West : *dans le restaurant Spice Route, on est assis sous des œuvres de sculpture sur bois et des peintures qui auraient leur place dans des musées. Les gourmets ont le choix entre quatre restaurants, deux bars et l'Atrium.*

Oriente y Occidente se saludan: *En el restaurante Spice Route uno se encuentra entre obras talladas y pinturas dignas de un museo. Los gourmets pueden elegir entre cuatro restaurantes, dos bares y el Atrium.*

East meets West: *nel ristorante Spice Route si sta seduti sotto intagli e quadri da museo. I palati fini hanno la scelta fra quattro ristoranti, due bar e il caffè dell'ingresso.*

Ananda in the Himalayas

Uttaranchal, India

In Sanskrit, Ananda means joy and contentment. In the cradle of Yoga and Ayurveda, the wellness resort has equally conquered the hearts of Hollywood and Bollywood greats. Art Deco lobby, library, billiards room, and the largest suites are accommodated in the Maharaja of Tehri-Garhwal's Moorish palace. The deluxe rooms lie in a new construction on the fringe of the nine-hole golf course high over Rishikesh. One even gazes over the holy Ganges River from the bathtub.

In Sanskrit bedeutet Ananda Freude und Zufriedenheit. An der Wiege von Yoga und Ayurveda hat das Wellness-Resort die Herzen von Hollywood- und Bollywood-Größen gleichermaßen erobert. Art déco-Lobby, Bibliothek, Billardzimmer und die größten Suiten sind in dem maurischen Palast des Maharadscha von Tehri-Garhwal untergebracht. Die De-Luxe-Räume liegen im Neubau am Rande des Neun-Loch Golfplatzes hoch über Rishikesh. Sogar von der Badewanne aus blickt man auf den heiligen Fluss Ganges.

En sanskrit, ananda signifie joie et satisfaction. Situé dans le berceau du yoga et de l'ayurveda, l'hôtel de tourisme wellness a conquis de la même manière les cœurs des grands de Hollywood et de Bollywood. Le hall en style art déco, la bibliothèque, la salle de billard et les plus grandes suites sont installées dans la palais maure du maharadjah de Tehri-Garhwal. Les pièces de luxe se trouvent dans le nouveau bâtiment près du terrain de golf à neuf trous surplombant Rishikesh. Même de la baignoire, on a vue sur le Gange, le fleuve sacré.

Ananda significa en sánscrito alegría y satisfacción. En la cuna del yoga y el Ayurveda este wellness resort ha conquistado por igual los corazones de los grandes de Hollywood y de Bollywood. El palacio moro del maharajá de Tehri-Garhwal alberga un vestíbulo Art Deco, biblioteca, salón de billar y las suites más amplias. Las habitaciones De-Luxe se encuentran en la nueva construcción al lado del campo de golf de nueve hoyos, en lo alto sobre Rishikesh. Incluso desde la bañera se tiene vista del sagrado Ganges.

Ananda in sanscrito significa gioia e beatitudine. Nella culla dello yoga e dell'ayurveda questo centro per il benessere ha conquistato il cuore dei grandi di Hollywood e di Bollywood. L'atrio in art déco, la biblioteca, la sala da bilardo e le più grandi suite sono sistemate nel palazzo moresco del maragià di Tehri-Garhwal. Le camere deluxe si trovano nell'edificio moderno ai margini del campo da golf a nove buche sopra Rishikesh. Persino dalla vasca da bagno si ha la vista sul fiume sacro, il Gange.

While bathing with attar of roses, during Ananda-Yoga, and during a relaxing massage, all the senses are revitalized.

Beim Bad mit Rosenöl, beim Ananda-Yoga und bei einer entspannenden Massage werden alle Sinne belebt.

Tous les sens sont éveillés lors d'un bain à l'huile de rose, de yoga ananda et d'un massage relaxant.

Los sentidos se estimulan con un baño de aceite de rosas, con una sesión de yoga ananda y con un relajante masaje.

Col bagno agli olii essenziali di rosa, con lo yoga ananda e con un massaggio rilassante vengono vivificati i sensi.

The interior *of the suites is inspired by the era of the Raj: framed, antique Jamawar cloths, teak beds, and noble baths.*

Das Interieur *der Suiten ist inspiriert von der Zeit der Raj: eingerahmte, antike Jamawar-Tücher, Teakbetten und edle Bäder.*

L'intérieur *des suites est inspiré de l'époque des Raj : tissus Jamawar antiques et encadrées, lits en teck et salles de bains splendides.*

La decoración interior *de las suites está inspirada en la época del Raj: Mantones Jamawar antiguos enmarcados, camas de madera de teca y elegantes baños.*

Gli interni *delle suite sono ispirati al tempo dei ragià: antiche stoffe jamawar incorniciate, letti in legno di tek e nobili bagni.*

Sunshine pours into the dining room and lobby through skylights. Sunbeds at the pool and small, quiet patios invite to relax.

Durch Oberlichter strömen Sonnenstrahlen in Speisesaal und Lobby. Zur Entspannung laden Liegen am Pool und kleine, ruhige Patios ein.

Les impostes permettent aux rayons du soleil d'inonder la salle à manger et le hall. Des chaises longues au bord de la piscine et de petits patios calmes invitent à la détente.

A través de las claraboyas fluyen los rayos de sol en el comedor y en el vestíbulo. Las tumbonas en la piscina y los pequeños y tranquilos patios invitan a relajarse.

Attraverso i lucernari i raggi di sole inondano sala da pranzo e atrio. I lettini della piscina e tranquilli cortiletti invitano al relax.

Rajvilas

Jaipur, India

Fairy-tale-like scenes hide behind fortress-like facades. Painted walls demonstrate Indian artisanship. Sculpted stucco formed from gypsum frames the windows and stone elephants spray fountains in the pool. The rooms open up to a romantic Mogul garden. Unforgettable: a night in the luxury tent. Teak wood furniture, Victorian bathtubs, and embroidered textiles are reminiscent of the carefree lives of Indian sovereigns, as is a dinner under the stars, to which Sitar music is played.

Hinter der festungsartigen Fassade verbergen sich Szenerien wie aus einem Märchen. Bemalte Wände demonstrieren indische Handwerkskunst. Stuckaturen aus Gips rahmen Fenster und steinerne Elefanten sprühen Fontänen in den Pool. Die Zimmer öffnen sich zu einem romantischen Mogul-Garten. Unvergesslich: eine Nacht im Luxus-Zelt. Teakholzmöbel, viktorianische Badewannen und bestickte Textilien erinnern an das sorglose Leben indischer Regenten – genau wie ein Dinner unter den Sternen, zu dem Sitar-Spieler musizieren.

Derrière la façade semblable à une forteresse se cachent des scénarios comme on pourrait en trouver dans les contes. Les murs peints représentent l'artisanat indien. Des stucs en plâtre encadrent les fenêtres et des éléphants en pierre font jaillir des jets d'eau dans la piscine. Les chambres s'ouvrent sur un romantique jardin Mogul. Inoubliable : une nuit dans la tente de luxe. Les meubles en bois teck, les baignoires victoriennes et les textiles brodés rappellent la vie insouciante des régents indiens – comme un dîner sous les étoiles lors duquel des musiciens jouent de la cithare.

Detrás de la fachada tipo fortaleza se esconden escenarios como de cuentos de hadas. Las paredes pintadas dan testimonio de la artesanía india. Trabajos en estuco de yeso enmarcan las ventanas y elefantes de piedra lanzan con sus surtidores agua a la piscina. Las habitaciones se abren hacia un romántico jardín mogol. Inolvidable: una noche en la tienda de campaña de lujo. Muebles de madera de teca, bañeras victorianas y tejidos bordados nos recuerdan la despreocupada vida de los soberanos indios –exactamente como una cena bajo las estrellas acompañada por la música de sitar.

Dietro la facciata a mo' di fortezza si celano scenari da fiaba. Pareti dipinte danno prova dell'artigianato artistico indiano. Stucchi di gesso incorniciano finestre ed elefanti di pietra spruzzano zampilli nella piscina. Le camere si aprono su un romantico giardino moghul. Indimenticabile: una notte nella tenda di lusso. Mobili in legno di tek, vasche da bagno vittoriane e tessuti ricamati rievocano la vita spensierata dei regnanti indiani – esattamente come una cena sotto le stelle, accompagnata da suonatori di sitar.

The hotel offers both traditional architecture in the lobby and facade, and modern marble baths with a view of the private garden.

Das Hotel bietet beides: Traditionelle Architektur in der Lobby und an der Fassade und moderne Marmorbäder mit Ausblick in den Privatgarten.

L'hôtel offre les deux : l'architecture traditionnelle dans le hall et sur la façade et des salles de bains modernes, en marbre, avec vue sur le jardin privé.

El hotel ofrece ambas cosas: Arquitectura tradicional en el vestíbulo y la fachada y baños modernos de mármol con vista al jardín privado.

L'hotel offre entrambe le cose: un'architettura tradizionale nell'ingresso e sulla facciata, ma anche bagni moderni in marmo con vista sui giardini privati.

Whether artistic carvings, *paintings, or elaborate ornamentation, Indian craftsmanship celebrates the love of detail.*

Ob Schnitzkunst, *Malerei oder kunstvolle Ornamentik – indische Handwerkskünste zelebrieren die Liebe zum Detail.*

Qu'il s'agisse de sculpture sur bois, *de peinture ou d'ornementation artistique – l'artisanat indien célèbre l'amour jusque dans le moindre détail.*

Sea en el arte de la talla, *la pintura o la ornamentación artística, la artesanía india celebra el amor al detalle.*

Non importa se intaglio, *pittura o arti ornamentali: i diversi rami dell'artigianato e dell'arte indiana celebrano l'amore per il dettaglio.*

The bath in a luxury tent *presents itself in a lovingly nostalgic way. In comparison, the sand colored facade seems defiantly fortified.*

Liebenswert-nostalgisch *präsentiert sich das Bad in einem der Luxuszelte, trutzig-wehrhaft dagegen die sandfarbene Fassade.*

La salle de bains *se présente sympathique et nostalgique dans l'une des tentes de luxe, la facade couleur sable est en revanche massive et vaillante.*

Encantadoramente nostálgico *es el baño en una de las tiendas de campaña de lujo; la fachada beige, por el contrario, da la sensación de una fortaleza.*

Amabilmente nostalgico *si presenta il bagno in una delle tende di lusso, simile a una tenda militare invece la facciata color sabbia.*

The Taj Mahal Palace & Tower

Mumbai, India

When the English architect W. Chambers built the hotel in 1903, it was incommensurable in the entire orient. Even today, the palace exudes its original charm; a mixture of English hospitality and Indian opulence: in the lobby, porters with turbans greet the guests, the suites in the old building are furnished with antiques, the corridors resemble art galleries. Modern urbanity joins traditional flair, such as in the Souk Restaurant or in Insomnia, Mumbai's largest nightclub.

Als der englische Architekt W. Chambers das Hotel 1903 erbaute, gab es im gesamten Orient nichts Vergleichbares. Noch heute versprüht der Palast seinen ursprünglichen Charme, einen Mix aus englischer Gastlichkeit und indischer Opulenz: In der Lobby empfangen Portiers mit Turbanen den Gast, die Suiten im alten Gebäude sind mit Antiquitäten ausgestattet, die Flure gleichen Kunstgalerien. Zum traditionellen Flair gesellt sich moderne Urbanität, wie in dem Restaurant Souk oder im Insomnia, Mumbais größtem Nachtclub.

Lorsque l'architecte anglais W. Chambers construisit l'hôtel en 1903, il n'existait rien de comparable dans tout l'Orient. Aujourd'hui encore, le palais déploie son charme d'origine, un mélange de convivialité anglaise et d'opulence indienne : dans le hall, des portiers avec des turbans accueillent l'hôtel, les suites dans l'ancien bâtiment sont aménagées d'antiquités, les couloirs ressemblent à des galeries d'art. Au flair traditionnel s'associe l'urbanité moderne, comme dans le restaurant Souk ou Insomnia, le plus grand club de nuit de Mumbai.

Cuando el arquitecto inglés W. Chambers construyó el hotel en 1903 no existía en todo el Oriente nada semejante. Aun hoy el palacio emana su encanto original, una combinación de hospitalidad inglesa y opulencia india: Porteros con turbantes reciben al huesped en el vestíbulo, las suites del edificio antiguo están decoradas con antigüedades, los pasillos parecen galerías de arte. Al ambiente tradicional se une lo moderno urbano, como en el restaurante Souk o en el Insomnia, el club nocturno más grande de Mumbai.

Quando l'architetto inglese W. Chambers edificò l'hotel nel 1903, in tutto l'Oriente non c'era nulla di paragonabile. Ancora oggi il palazzo sprizza del suo fascino originario, un misto di ospitalità inglese e opulenza indiana: all'ingresso portieri in turbante accolgono gli ospiti, le suite nell'edificio antico sono arredate con pezzi di antiquariato, i corridoi assomigliano a gallerie d'arte. Al flair tradizionale si accompagna l'urbanità moderna, come nel ristorante Souk o nell'Insomnia, il più grande night-club di Mumbai.

Even just the stairway in the stately Victorian building is a worthy attraction. The swimming pool is located in the inner courtyard; the Sea Lounge is a favorite meeting point for society.

Alleine schon das Treppenhaus des viktorianischen Prachtbaus ist eine Sehenswürdigkeit, im Innenhof befindet sich das Schwimmbad, beliebter Treffpunkt der Gesellschaft ist die Sea Lounge.

Rien que la cage d'escalier du superbe bâtiment victorien est une curiosité, la piscine se trouve dans la cour intérieure, le point de rencontre préféré de la société est le Sea Lounge.

La escalera de la magnífica construcción victoriana ya es de por sí un monumento. En el patio interior se encuentra la piscina; punto favorito de encuentro de la alta sociedad es el Sea Lounge.

Già solo la scalinata del sontuoso edificio vittoriano è una bellezza da vedere, nel cortile interno si trova la piscina, popolare luogo d'incontro dell'élite locale è il Sea Lounge.

Nine bars and restaurants and the minimalist designed nightclub are spread around the old palace and the new high-rise.

Neun Bars und Restaurants sowie der minimalistisch gestaltete Nachtclub verteilen sich über den alten Palast und das neuere Hochhaus.

Neuf bars et restaurants, ainsi que le club de nuit à la réalisation minimaliste sont répartis sur l'ancien palais et le building le plus récent.

Nueve bares y restaurantes, así como el club nocturno de estilo minimalista, se encuentran repartidos entre el viejo palacio y la nueva edificación.

Nove bar e ristoranti, nonché il night-club dall'arredo minimalistico, sono distribuiti tra il palazzo vecchio e il nuovo grattacielo.

A tour through the hotel is like a trip back through time to the British colonial era up through present day India. In total, there are 546 rooms including 49 suites.

Ein Rundgang durch das Hotel gleicht einer Zeitreise von der britischen Kolonialzeit bis in die indische Gegenwart. Insgesamt gibt es 546 Zimmer inklusive 49 Suiten.

Un tour dans l'hôtel ressemble à un voyage dans le temps, de l'époque coloniale britannique à l'époque actuelle indienne. Il y a au total 546 chambres, y compris 49 suites.

Una vuelta por el hotel parece un viaje a través del tiempo, desde la época colonial británica hasta la India actual. En total hay 546 habitaciones, incluyendo 49 suites.

Un giro per l'hotel assomiglia a un viaggio nel tempo, dall'epoca coloniale britannica fino al presente indiano. Nel complesso ci sono 546 camere, incluse le 49 suite.

Intercontinental Marine Drive

Mumbai, India

A design-oriented hotel was what was missing from the megacity's center. In the suites in the structure from the turn of the century, comfort is combined with the newest high-tech. Businessmen and women recuperate in the Bar Czar with a whiskey. Whoever prefers sunset should try the Dome, the roof terrace lounge. Mumbai's scene enjoys the view of the glittering inlet.

Ein designorientiertes Hotel hat im Zentrum der Megacity gefehlt. In den Suiten des Jahrhundertwende-Baus wird Komfort spielerisch mit neuestem Hightech kombiniert. Geschäftsleute erholen sich in der Bar Czar beim Whiskey. Wer den Sonnenuntergang bevorzugt, ist im Dome richtig, der Dachterrassen-Lounge. Hier genießt Mumbais Szene die Aussicht auf die glitzernde Bucht.

Un hôtel mettant l'accent sur le design manquait dans le centre de la mégacité. Dans les suites du bâtiment datant du tournant du siècle, le confort est associé avec désinvolture à la haute technologie la plus récente. Les hommes d'affaires se reposent au bar Czar devant un whiskey. Celui qui préfère le coucher de soleil, se trouve à la bonne place dans le Dome, le salon sur les toits en terrasse. Ici, la scène de Mumbai profite de la vue sur la baie scintillante.

En el centro de esta megaciudad hacía falta un hotel orientado hacia el diseño. En las suites de esta construcción de fin de siglo se combinan sin dificultad el confort y la más moderna tecnología. Los hombres y mujeres de negocios se recuperan bebiendo un whisky en el bar Czar. Para quien prefiere la puesta del sol, lo acertado es el Dome, el lounge de la azotea. Aquí disfruta la jet set de Mumbai de la vista de la bahía resplandeciente.

Un hotel griffato mancava nel centro della megacity. Nelle suite dell'edificio a cavallo dei due secoli il comfort si combina con facilità con l'high tech dell'ultima ora. Uomini d'affari si rilassano nel bar Czar davanti a un whisky. Chi preferisce il tramonto del sole è al suo posto nel Dome, lounge con terrazza sul tetto. Qui l'élite di Mumbai gode della vista sulla baia scintillante.

Traditional Indian decor and works of art were deftly integrated into the modern interior of the lobby.

Traditionelles indisches Dekor und Kunstwerke wurden geschickt in das moderne Interieur der Lobby integriert.

Décor et œuvres d'art indiens traditionnels ont été intégrés avec habileté à l'intérieur moderne du hall.

Artesanía india tradicional y obras de arte han sido integradas hábilmente en el interior moderno del vestíbulo.

Il tradizionale décor indiano e le opere d'arte sono state sapientemente integrate nell'interno moderno dell'ingresso.

From the pool on the roof, the view reaches over the sweeping inlet, called "The Queens Necklace". Cosmopolitan elegance characterizes the restaurant and bar.

Vom Pool auf dem Dach reicht der Blick über die geschwungene Bucht, genannt „The Queens Necklace". Weltstädtische Eleganz prägen Restaurant und Bar.

De la piscine sur le toit, on a vue sur la baie traçant des courbes, appelée « The Queens Necklace ». L'élégance d'une grande ville de renommée mondiale caractérise le restaurant et le bar.

Desde la piscina de la azotea la vista llega hasta la ondulada bahía, llamada "El collar de la reina". El restaurante y el bar se caracterizan por su elegancia cosmopolita.

Dalla piscina sul tetto lo sguardo si estende sulla baia arcuata, chiamata "The Queens Necklace". Eleganza cosmopolita caratterizza bar e ristorante.

The gentle color pallet of the suites calms the senses after a day in the pulsing city of over a million inhabitants. The sofas on the roof terrace are ideal for a sundowner.

Die sanfte Farbpalette der Suiten beruhigt die Sinne nach einem Tag in der pulsierenden Millionenstadt. Ideal für einen Sundowner sind die begehrten Sofas auf der Dachterrasse.

La douce palette de couleurs des suites calme les sens après une journée dans la ville bouillonnante. Les canapés très convoités sur le toit en terrasse sont l'idéal pour un sundowner.

La suave gama de colores de las suites relaja los sentidos después de un día en la vibrante ciudad de más de diez millones de habitantes. Ideales para disfrutar un sundowner son los codiciados sofás de la azotea.

La tavolozza dei colori tenui delle suite acquieta i sensi dopo un giorno nella pulsante metropoli. Ideali per un sundowner sono i ricercati sofà della terrazza sul tetto.

Devi Garh

Udaipur, India

A fairy-tale castle rises in the hills of Rajasthan. Behind the towers of the fortress from 1760, the owner Lekha Poddar has created refreshing minimalism. In the white walls, malachite and lapis lazuli set varied dabs of color, silk scarves shine in front of the windows in pink and orange. A marble pool and sundeck seduce one into doing nothing. And mirrors twinkle like stars on the canvas roof of the seven luxury tents.

In den Hügeln Rajasthans erhebt sich ein Märchenschloss. Hinter den Türmen der Festung von 1760 hat die Besitzerin Lekha Poddar erfrischenden Minimalismus geschaffen. In den weißen Mauern setzen Malachit und Lapislazuli bunte Farbtupfer, vor den Fenstern leuchten Seidenschals in Pink und Orange. Ein Marmor-Pool und Sonnendecks verführen zum Nichtstun. Und Spiegel blinken wie Sterne auf dem Canvas-Dach der sieben Luxus-Zelte.

Au milieu des collines du Rajasthan s'élève un château de contes. Derrière les tours de la forteresse de 1760, la propriétaire Lekha Poddar a créé un minimalisme rafraîchissant. Dans les murs blancs, le malachit et le lapis lazuli posent des touches de couleur bigarrées, des écharpes en soie rose et orange brillent devant les fenêtres. Une piscine en marbre et des ponts supérieurs invitent au farniente. Et des miroirs brillent comme des étoiles sur le toit Canvas des sept tentes de luxe.

En las colinas de Rajastán se yergue un castillo de cuentos de hadas. Detrás de las torres de la fortaleza de 1760 la propietaria Lekha Poddar ha creado un minimalismo reconfortante. En los muros blancos las malaquitas y el lapislázuli ponen notas de color, ante las ventanas resplandecen pañuelos de seda rosados y naranjas. Una piscina de mármol y cubiertas para tomar el sol, incitan al ocio. Y los espejos brillan como estrellas en el techo de lona de las siete lujosas tiendas de campaña.

Sulle colline del Rajasthan si erge un castello da fiaba. Dietro le torri della fortezza del 1760 la proprietaria Lekha Poddar ha imposto un minimalismo brioso. Sui muri bianchi malachite e lapislazuli fanno colore, davanti alle finestre rispledono foulard di seta in rosa e in arancio. Una piscina di marmo e solarium istigano a non fare nulla. E sulla copertura canvas delle sette tende di lusso degli specchi luccicano come stelle.

While the castle outside is resplendent with decorations of sand and ocher hues, the interior rooms are kept minimalist in white and pastel colors.

Während der Palast von außen mit opulentem Dekor in Sand- und Ockertönen prunkt, sind die Innenräume minimalistisch in Weiß und Pastellfarben gehalten.

Alors que le palais brille de l'extérieur avec un décor opulent dans les tons sable et ocre, les pièces intérieures sont restées minimalistes en blanc et en couleur pastel.

Mientras que por fuera el palacio resplandece con opulencia en tonos beige y ocres, los espacios interiores están diseñados en blanco y tonos pasteles en un estilo minimalista.

Mentre il palazzo troneggia all'esterno con l'opulenta decorazione in tonalità sabbia e ocra, gli ambienti interni sono sistemati minimalisticamente in bianco e nei colori pastello.

Regardless whether in one of the lounges, in the romantic courtyards or at the pool: one finds new, fascinating perspectives all around.

Egal, ob in einer der Lounges, in romantischen Innenhöfen oder am Pool: überall findet man neue, faszinierende Blickwinkel.

Que cela soit dans l'un des salons, dans les cours intérieures romantiques ou au bord de la piscine : on trouve partout de nouveaux angles de vue fascinants.

Sea en uno de los lounges, en uno de los románticos patios interiores o en la piscina: Por todas partes se encuentran ángulos fascinantes.

In uno dei lounge, nei romantici cortili interni o in piscina fa lo stesso: dappertutto si trovano nuove, affascinanti prospettive.

Devi Garh *Udaipur, India* 47

With the exemplarily successful transformation of the Maharaja Palace into a boutique-hotel, Devi Garh has become the epitome of modern Indian lifestyle in the meantime.

Mit der beispielhaft gelungenen Umwandlung des Maharadscha-Palastes in ein Boutiquehotel ist Devi Garh inzwischen zum Inbegriff des modernen, indischen Lebensstils geworden.

Avec la transformation exemplaire et réussie du palais du maharadjah en un hôtel boutique, Devi Garh est entre-temps devenu le symbole du style de vie moderne indien.

Con la lograda y ejemplar transformación del palacio del maharajá en un hotel boutique, el Devi Garh se ha convertido en la quintaesencia del estilo de vida moderno indio.

Con la ben riuscita trasformazione del palazzo del Maragià in un hotel esclusivo, Devi Garh è diventato la quintessenza dello stile di vita moderno indiano.

Udaivilas

Udaipur, India

Elephants made out of marble flank the entrance to a magical world: golden domes crown arcades, fountains bubble in the lobby, lotus blossoms adorn the pool. The hotel reflects the lifestyle of the Maharajas in all facets. Thecomplex stretches along Lake Pichola to the former hunting grounds of the Mewar Kingdom. In the suites, oriels offer dreamlike views of the lake. Even telescopes stand ready to observe every detail of the city palace facing opposite.

Elefanten aus Marmor flankieren den Eingang zu einer Wunderwelt: Goldene Kuppeln krönen Arkaden, Fontänen sprudeln in der Lobby, Lotusblüten zieren den Pool. Das Hotel spiegelt den Lebensstil der Maharadschas in allen Facetten wider. Die Anlage erstreckt sich entlang des Pichola-Sees auf den ehemaligen Jagdgründen des Königreichs Mewar. In den Suiten bieten Erker traumhafte Ausblicke auf den See. Selbst Teleskope stehen bereit, um jedes Detail des gegenüberliegenden City Palace zu betrachten.

L'entrée dans un monde merveilleux est flanquée d'éléphants en marbre : des coupoles dorées couronnent les arcades, des fontaines bouillonnent dans le hall, des fleurs de lotus ornent la piscine. L'hôtel reflète le style de vie des maharadjahs dans toutes ses facettes. Le site s'étend le long du lac Pichola sur les anciens terrains de chasse du royaume Mewar. Dans les suites, les encorbellements donnent des vues de rêve sur le lac. Même des télescopes sont installés pour observer chaque détail du City Palace situé en face.

Elefantes de mármol flanquean la entrada hacia un mundo maravilloso: Cúpulas doradas coronan las arcadas, fuentes burbujean en el vestíbulo, flores de loto adornan la piscina. El hotel refleja el estilo de vida del maharajá en todas sus facetas. El complejo hotelero se extiende a lo largo del lago Pichola en los antiguos terrenos de caza del reino Mewar. En las suites los miradores ofrecen vistas maravillosas del lago. Incluso hay telescopios listos para observar cada detalle del City Palace situado enfrente.

Elefanti di marmo fiancheggiano l'entrata in un mondo fantastico: cupole dorate coronano portici, fontane a getto zampillano nell'atrio, fiori di loto adornano la piscina. L'hotel riflette in tutte le sfacettature lo stile di vita dei maragià. La costruzione si estende lungo il lago Pichola sugli ex territori di caccia del regno del Mewar. Nelle suite i bovindo offrono vedute da sogno sul lago. Sono a disposizione persino dei telescopi, per contemplare ogni dettaglio del City Palace che sta di fronte.

Indian ornaments are reflected in the lobby's fountain and in the pool.

Im Springbrunnen der Lobby und im Pool spiegeln sich die indischen Ornamente.

Dans le jet d'eau du hall et dans la piscine se reflètent les ornementations indiennes.

En las fuentes del vestíbulo y en la piscina se reflejan los ornamentos indios.

Nelle fontane a getto dell'atrio e nella piscina si specchiano le decorazioni indiane.

At twilight, hundreds of lights and candles bathe the arcades, terraces and pools in a magical luster.

In der Dämmerung tauchen Hunderte von Lichtern und Kerzen die Arkaden, Terrassen und Pools in magischen Glanz.

Au crépuscule, des centaines de lumières et de bougies plongent les arcades, les terrasses et les piscines dans un éclat magique.

A la hora del crepúsculo aparecen con mágico resplandor cientos de luces y velas en las arcadas, las terrazas y piscinas.

All'imbrunire centinaia di luci e di candele immergono i portici, le terrazze e le piscine in un magico splendore.

A hand painted, richly decorated elephant adorns the wall in the nostalgic bathroom, colorful pillows bedeck the cozy oriels in the luxury suites.

Ein handgemalter, reich geschmückter Elefant ziert die Wand im nostalgischen Bad, bunte Kissen die gemütlichen Erker der Luxussuiten.

Un éléphant richement décoré et peint à la main orne le mur dans la salle de bains nostalgique, des coussins colorés décorent les encorbellements confortables des suites de luxe.

Un elefante pintado a mano y decorado suntuosamente adorna la pared en el nostálgico baño, y cojines de colores los acogedores miradores de las suites.

Un elefante dipinto a mano, riccamente addobbato, decora la parete nel bagno nostalgico, cuscini colorati adornano gli accoglienti bovindo delle suite di lusso.

The Strand

Yangon, Myanmar

In 1901, the hotel opened its gates for the first time and the charm of times past is still maintained after an extensive renovation in the mid-nineties. 32 up to 200 m² suites with 3.50 m ceilings await the guest: warm wooden floors, ocher colored walls, natural-colored fabrics and large baths with fine tile patterns impart a feeling of living as in the time the hotel first emerged under British colonial rule.

1901 öffnete das Hotel erstmals seine Pforten und der Charme vergangener Zeiten ist auch nach einer umfangreichen Renovierung Mitte der Neunziger Jahre erhalten geblieben. 32 bis zu 200 m² große Suiten mit 3,50 m hohen Decken erwarten den Gast: Warme Holzfußböden, ockerfarbene Wände, naturfarbene Stoffe und große Bäder mit feinen Fliesenmustern vermitteln ihm ein Wohngefühl wie zur Entstehungszeit des Hotels unter britischer Kolonialherrschaft.

C'est en 1901 que l'hôtel a ouvert pour la première fois ses portes et le charme des temps passés est toujours conservé, même après une importante rénovation effectuée au milieu des années quatre-vingt dix. 32 grande suites jusqu'à 200 m² avec des plafonds d'une hauteur de 3,50 m attendent l'hôte : le plancher chaud en bois, des murs de couleur ocre, des tissus couleur nature et de grandes salles de bains avec de délicats motifs de carreaux lui donnent la sensation d'habiter à l'époque de la fondation de l'hôtel sous la souveraineté coloniale britannique.

El hotel abrió sus puertas por primera vez en 1901 y aun después de una extensa remodelación a mediados de los años 90 conserva el encanto de épocas pasadas. 32 suites de hasta 200 m², con techos de 3,50 metros de altura, esperan al huesped: Suelos de madera cálidos, paredes en tono ocre, telas de color natural y baños espaciosos con finos diseños de baldosas, transmiten al huésped la sensación de vivir en la época del dominio colonial británico, cuando se fundó el hotel.

L'hotel aprì per la prima volta i battenti nel 1901, ma il fascino dei tempi passati è rimasto intatto anche dopo una grossa ristrutturazione a metà degli anni Novanta. Attendono l'ospite 32 suite grandi fino a 200 m² con soffitti alti 3,50 m: caldi pavimenti di legno, pareti color ocra, stoffe dai colori naturali e grandi bagni con piastrelle dai disegni raffinati gli trasmettono una sensazione di accoglienza come all'epoca in cui sorse l'hotel sotto il dominio britannico.

The atmosphere of a hotel with over one-hundred years tradition cannot only be felt in the Strand bar.

Die Atmosphäre eines Hotels mit über hundertjähriger Tradition ist nicht nur in der „Strand"-Bar zu spüren.

L'ambiance d'un hôtel à la tradition de plus de cent ans ne se ressent pas seulement dans le bar Strand.

La atmósfera de un hotel con más de un siglo de tradición no sólo se nota en el bar Strand.

L'atmosfera di un hotel di tradizione ultracentenaria si può sentire non soltanto nel bar Strand.

One *reaches the suites via the corridors in the three-storey atrium.*

Über *die Flure des dreigeschossigen Atrium gelangt man in die Suiten.*

On *a accès aux suites par les couloirs de l'atrium à trois étages.*

Por *los corredores del atrio de tres pisos se llega a las suites.*

Dai *corridoi dell'atrio centrale a tre piani si raggiungono le suite.*

The Sukhothai

Bangkok, Thailand

Walls covered with Thai silk, miniature temples in water basins, canopy beds—the architect Kerry Hill and the star interior architect Ed Tuttle have managed to unite oriental opulence with western minimalism behind the unflourished facade. The team placed special value on haptic charms: textures such as linen, waffle piqué, porous stones and granite in the suites are meant to sharpen the senses, just like the artistically arranged dishes in the Celadon Restaurant.

Mit Thai-Seide bespannte Wände, Miniatur-Tempel in Wasserbassins, Baldachin-Betten – dem Architekten Kerry Hill und dem Star-Innenarchitekt Ed Tuttle ist es gelungen, hinter der schnörkellosen Fassade orientalische Opulenz mit westlichem Minimalismus zu vereinen. Besonderen Wert legte das Team auf haptische Reize: Texturen wie Leinen, Waffelpiqué, poröse Steine und Granit in den Suiten sollen die Sinne schärfen, genauso wie die kunstvoll arrangierten Speisen im Restaurant Celadon.

Avec des murs recouverts de soie Thaï, des temples miniatures dans des bassins d'eau, des lits à baldaquin, l'architecte Kerry Hill et l'architecte d'intérieur en vogue Ed Tuttle ont réussi à unifier derrière la façade sans fioritures l'opulence orientale au minimalisme occidental. L'équipe accorda une valeur particulière aux charmes haptiques : des textures comme le lin, le gaufré piqué, des pierres poreuses et du granit dans les suites sont censés aiguiser les sens, comme les repas arrangés avec bon goût au restaurant Celadon.

Paredes revestidas de seda tailandesa, templos en miniatura en los depósitos de agua, camas con doseles –el arquitecto Kerry Hill y el diseñador de interiores Ed Tuttle han conseguido unir detrás de una fachada sin adornos la opulencia oriental con el minimalismo occidental. El equipo dio especial importancia a la estimulación del tacto: En las suites las texturas como el lino, el piqué, las piedra porosas y el granito aguzarán los sentidos, al igual que los platos servidos artísticamente en el restaurante Celadon.

Con pareti rivestite di seta tailandese, templi in miniatura in bacini d'acqua, letti a baldacchino, l'architetto Kerry Hill e la star dell'architetura di interni Ed Tuttle sono riusciti, dietro la facciata senza fronzoli, a unire opulenza orientale e minimalismo occidentale. Il team ha dato particolare valore agli stimoli tattili: i tessuti in lino, a nido d'ape, le pietre porose e il granito nelle suite devono affinare i sensi, così come i cibi disposti ad arte nel ristorante Celadon.

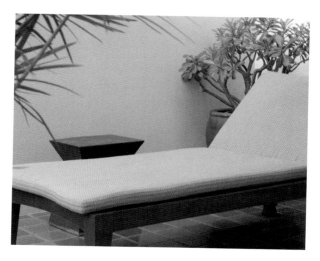

The emphatically minimalist facade rises above the pool terrace.

Über der Pool-Terrasse erhebt sich die betont minimalistische Fassade.

La façade au minimalisme prononcé s'élève au-dessus de la terrasse de la piscine.

Sobre la piscina de la azotea se levanta la fachada de carácter marcadamente minimalista.

Sopra la terrazza della piscina si eleva la facciata marcatamanete minimalistica.

The lobby atrium presents itself festively elegant. The suites are furnished with finest Thai silk.

Festlich-elegant präsentiert sich das Atrium der Lobby. Die Suiten sind mit feinster Thai-Seide ausgestattet.

L'atrium du hall se présente festif et élégant. Les suites sont aménagées avec de la soie Thaï extrêmement délicate.

El atrio del vestíbulo se presenta festivo y elegante. Las suites están decoradas con la más fina seda tailandesa.

L'atrio dell'ingresso si presenta solenne ed elegante. Le suite sono arredate con le più fini sete tailandesi.

Water surfaces *as smooth as glass reflect the evocative evening lighting. The hotel restaurants are considered gourmet temples by insiders and tourists.*

Spiegelglatte Wasserflächen *reflektieren die stimmungsvolle Abendbeleuchtung. Die Restaurants des Hotels gelten als Gourmettempel bei Insidern und Touristen.*

La surface de l'eau, *lisse comme un miroir, est mise en valeur par l'éclairage nocturne évocateur. Les restaurants de l'hôtel passent pour être des temples de gourmets chez les initiés et les touristes.*

Superficies de agua, *lisas como espejos, reflejan la acogedora iluminación nocturna. Los restaurantes son considerados templos gourmet entre los entendidos y los turistas.*

Le superfici d'acqua, *lisce come specchi, riflettono la suggestiva illuminazione notturna. I ristoranti dell'hotel passano per templi del buon gusto sia per insider che per turisti.*

The Oriental
Bangkok, Thailand

On Chao Phrya, the river that winds through the metropolis like a snake looms The Oriental. For over a century, literary figures from around the world have let themselves be inspired by the atmosphere. The suites in the Authors Wing are homage to famous authors and attuned to them: wooden wainscoting and a nautical flair for Captain Anderson, colonial style with teak and silk for the novelist Wilbur Smith, pink damask for the romancière Barbara Cartland.

Am Chao Phrya, dem Fluss, der sich wie eine Schlange durch die Metropole windet, ragt The Oriental auf. Über ein Jahrhundert lang haben sich Literaten aus aller Welt von der Atmosphäre des Hotels inspirieren lassen. Die Suiten im Authors Wing sind eine Hommage an berühmte Schriftsteller und auf sie abgestimmt: Holzvertäfelung und nautisches Flair für Kapitän Anderson, Kolonialstil mit Teak und Seide für Novellist Wilbur Smith, rosa Damast für Romancière Barbara Cartland.

The Oriental se dresse le long du Chao Phrya, le fleuve qui se contorsionne tel un serpent à travers la métropole. Pendant plus d'un siècle, les gens de lettres du monde entier se sont laissés inspirer par l'atmosphère de l'hôtel. Les suites dans l'aile des auteurs sont un hommage aux écrivains célèbres et réalisés à leur mesure : boiseries et flair nautique pour le capitaine Anderson, style colonial en teck et soie pour le nouvelliste Wilbur Smith, damas rose pour la romancière Barbara Cartland.

A orillas del Chao Phrya, el río que se desliza como una serpiente por la metrópoli, sobresale el Oriental. Por más de un siglo se inspiraron en el ambiente del hotel escritores de todo el mundo. Las suites en el ala de los autores son un homenaje a escritores famosos y de acuerdo a ellos están decoradas: Revestimiento de madera y aire náutico, para el Capitán Anderson; estilo colonial con madera de teca y seda, para el novelista Wilbur Smith; damasco rosado, para la novelista Barbara Cartland.

Sul Chao Phrya, il fiume che si snoda come un serpente per la metropoli, si erge The Oriental. Per più di un secolo letterati di tutto il mondo si sono lasciati ispirare dalle atmosfere dell'hotel. Le suite nell'ala degli autori sono un omaggio ai famosi scrittori a cui sono dedicate: rivestimenti in legno e flair nautico per il capitano Anderson, stile coloniale in tek e seta per il novellista Wilbur Smith, damasco rosa per la scrittrice Barbara Cartland.

A section of the world's most highly awarded hotel lies on the other side of the river. A ferry brings the guests to the legendary spa, to the Thai restaurant Sala Rim Naam or to the chef's school.

Ein Teil des am meisten ausgezeichneten Hotels der Welt liegt auf der anderen Seite des Flusses. Ein Pendelboot bringt die Gäste ins legendäre Spa, ins Thai Restaurant Sala Rim Naam oder in die Kochschule.

Une partie de cet hôtel qui a reçu le plus de distinctions dans le monde se trouve de l'autre côté du fleuve. Un bateau navette emmène les hôtes au spa, au restaurant Thaï Sala Rim Naam ou à l'école de cuisine.

El hotel, que cuenta con más distinciones en el mundo que cualquier otro, tiene una parte de sus instalaciones al otro lado del río. Un bote transporta a los huéspedes al Spa, al restaurante de comida tailandesa Sala Rim Naam o a la escuela de cocina.

Una parte dell'hotel più premiato del mondo si trova sull'altra riva del fiume. Un'imbarcazione fa da spola per portare gli ospiti alle terme, al ristorante tailandese Sala Rim Naam o alla scuola di cucina.

Choice collector's items, *noble period furniture, and historic atmosphere: a walk through the hotel resembles a visit to an antique dealer.*

Ausgesuchte Sammlerstücke, *edle Stilmöbel und historische Atmosphäre: Der Gang durch das Hotel gleicht dem Besuch eines Antiquitätengeschäfts.*

Des pièces de collection choisies, *de beaux meubles stylés et une atmosphère historique : le tour de l'hôtel ressemble à la visite d'un magasin d'antiquité.*

Piezas de colección exclusivas, *finos muebles de época y un ambiente histórico: Un recorrido por el hotel parece la visita a una tienda de antigüedades.*

Pezzi scelti da collezione, *preziosi mobili in stile e un'atmosfera storica: fare un giro per l'hotel è come andare in un negozio di antiquariato.*

A legend in all aspects: not only famous guests characterized and set the tone of the hotel: after 36 years of service, director Kurt Wachtveitl himself has become a legend in the hotel branch. No one has ever managed a hotel for so long.

Eine Legende in jeder Beziehung: Nicht nur die berühmten Gäste prägten und prägen das Haus; Direktor Kurt Wachtveitl ist nach 36 Dienstjahren selbst zur Legende der Hotelbranche geworden. Noch nie hat jemand so lange ein Hotel geleitet.

Une légende à tous égards : ce ne sont pas seulement les hôtes célèbres qui ont marqué et qui marquent la maison ; le directeur Kurt Wachtveitl est passé lui-même dans la légende de la branche des hôtels après 36 années de service. Personne n'a encore dirigé aussi longtemps un hôtel.

Una leyenda en todo sentido: No sólo los huéspedes famosos caracterizaron y caracterizan el hotel. El mismo director, Kurt Wachtveitl, es después de 36 años de servicio una leyenda en el ámbito hotelero. Nunca antes había alguien dirigido durante tanto tiempo un hotel.

Una leggenda da ogni punto di vista: non solo gli ospiti famosi hanno plasmato e plasmano il carattere della casa, il direttore stesso Kurt Wachtveitl è diventato la leggenda del settore dopo 36 anni di servizio. Mai nessuno prima ha diretto così a lungo un hotel.

Four Seasons Resort Chiang Mai

Chiang Mai, Thailand

The resort is formed like a horseshoe around a rice plantation, allowing the region's typical landscape to be experienced in all its buildings. Its 64 pavilion and 16 residence suites are erected on stakes and, in part, the terraces loom directly over the fields. The facility's design is oriented on the in northern Thailand predominant Lanna architecture with its filigree timber construction, the small landing stages, bridges, oriels, and steeply pitched roofs.

Das Resort ist in Form eines Hufeisens um eine Reisplantage herum angelegt, sodass sich das typische Landschaftsbild der Region in allen Gebäuden erleben lässt. Seine 64 Pavillon- und 16 Residenz-Suiten sind auf Pfählen errichtet, und die Terrassen ragen zum Teil direkt über die Felder. Gestalterisch orientiert sich die Anlage an der im nördlichen Thailand vorherrschenden Lanna-Architektur mit ihrer filigranen Holzbauweise, den kleinen Stegen, Brücken, Erkern und spitz zulaufenden Steildächern.

L'hôtel de tourisme a la forme d'un fer à cheval situé autour d'une plantation de riz, si bien qu'il est possible de profiter du paysage typique de la région dans tous les bâtiments. Ses 64 suites de pavillon et 16 suites de résidence sont construites sur des pieux et les terrasses s'élèvent en partie directement au-dessus des champs. Du point de vue de la réalisation, le site s'inspire de l'architecture Lanna dominante en Thaïlande du nord – avec son style de construction en bois filigrane, les petites passerelles, les ponts, les encorbellements et les toits pentus et pointus.

El resort está construido en forma de herradura alrededor de una plantación de arroz, de tal manera que el típico paisaje de la región se puede apreciar desde cualquiera de las edificaciones. Sus 64 suites pabellón y las 16 tipo residencia están erigidas sobre pilotes y las terrazas, en parte, se elevan directamente sobre los campos. El estilo del complejo está basado en la arquitectura Lanna, predominante en el Norte de Tailandia, con sus delicadas y pulidas construcciones de madera, los pequeños senderos, puentes, miradores y tejados inclinados.

Il resort è stato tracciato a forma di ferro di cavallo intorno a una piantagione di riso, in modo che si possa vivere il tipico paesaggio della regione in tutti gli edifici. Le ottanta suite – 64 padiglioni e 16 residence – sono costruite su palafitte e le terrazze sporgono in parte direttamente sui campi. Il complesso si orienta in modo creativo all'architettura lanna che domina il nord della Tailandia con gli edifici di legno in filigrana, le passerelle, i ponti, i bovindo e i tetti a spiovente che terminano a punta.

Ceilings opening toward the top ensure well-balanced air circulation in the bedrooms.

In den Schlafräumen sorgen nach oben offene Decken für eine ausgeglichene Luftzirkulation.

Dans les chambres à coucher, les plafonds ouverts vers le haut garantissent une circulation équilibrée de l'air.

En las habitaciones se logra una constante circulación de aire gracias a la apertura de los techos.

Nelle camere da letto i tetti aperti verso l'alto fanno sì che ci sia un'equilibrata circolazione dell'aria.

The luscious green surroundings are present throughout the resort. When the weather is clear, even the Doi Suthep Pui Mountains can be seen.

Die saftig grüne Umgebung ist im gesamten Resort präsent. Bei klarem Wetter sind sogar die Doi Suthep Pui Berge zu sehen.

L'environnement de couleur vert intense est présent dans la totalité de l'hôtel de tourisme. Par temps clair, il est même possible de voir les montagnes Doi Suthep Pui.

La abundante vegetación del entorno está siempre presente en el resort. Cuando está despejado se pueden ver incluso las montañas Doi Suthep Pui.

Il verde intenso dell'ambiente circostante è presente in tutto il resort. Quando l'aria è nitida si possono persino vedere i monti Doi Suthep Pui.

Raffles Hotel Le Royal

Phnom Penh, Cambodia

With its mixture of Khmer architecture and French colonialism, the hotel built in 1929 counts among those legendary in Indochina. The original buildings and an extension adaptation on the original are grouped around both pools in a tropical garden. Along with 208 rooms and suites, there are three restaurants, a café and the Elephant Bar, in Phnom Penh once again a genuine institution.

Mit seiner Mischung aus Khmer-Architektur und französischem Kolonialismus zählt das 1929 erbaute Hotel zu den Legenden Indochinas. Um die beiden Pools in einem tropischen Garten gruppieren sich das ursprüngliche Gebäude und eine dem Original nachempfundene Erweiterung. Darin befinden sich neben 208 Zimmern und Suiten insgesamt auch drei Restaurants, ein Café und die Elephant Bar, in Phnom Penh heute wieder eine echte Institution.

Avec son mélange d'architecture Khmer et de colonialisme français, l'hôtel construit en 1929 compte parmi les légendes d'Indochine. Autour des deux piscines dans un jardin tropical se groupent le bâtiment d'origine et une extension inspirée de l'original. En plus des 208 chambres et suites se trouvent au total également trois restaurants, un café et le bar Elephant, aujourd'hui redevenu à Phnom Penh une véritable institution.

Con su combinación de arquitectura Khmer y colonialismo francés, el hotel construido en 1929, se cuenta entre las leyendas de Indochina. Alrededor de las dos piscinas ubicadas en medio de un jardín tropical se agrupan la construcción original y una ampliación hecha a su semejanza. Allí se encuentran junto a las 208 habitaciones y suites también tres restaurantes, un café y el bar Elefante, hoy en día nuevamente una verdadera institución en Phnom Penh.

Con la sua mescolanza di architettura Khmer e stile coloniale francese, l'hotel costruito nel 1929 viene annoverato tra le leggende dell'Indocina. Intorno alle due piscine poste in un giardino tropicale sono raggruppati l'edificio originario e un ampliamento ispirato all'originale. Qui si trovano, accanto alle complessive 208 camere e suite, anche tre ristoranti, un caffè e il bar Elephant, oggi di nuovo una vera istituzione a Phnom Penh.

The hotel, reminiscent of a palace, lies in the center of Phnom Penh.

Das an einen Palast erinnernde Hotel liegt im Zentrum von Phnom Penh.

L'hôtel, qui rappelle un palais, se trouve au centre de Phnom Penh.

El hotel, que recuerda un palacio, se encuentra en el centro de Phnom Penh.

L'hotel, che ricorda piuttosto un palazzo, si trova nel centro di Phnom Penh.

Festive dinner in Restaurant Le Royal or relaxation on one of the two pools; both are tied closely together here.

Festliches Dinner im Restaurant Le Royal oder Entspannung an einem der beiden Pools; beides gehört hier eng zusammen.

Dîner de façon festive au restaurant Le Royal ou se détendre au bord de l'une des deux piscines ; les deux sont ici étroitement liés.

Cena festiva en el restaurante Le Royal o relajamiento en una de las dos piscinas; aquí ambas actividades se compaginan muy bien.

Un pasto magnifico al ristorante Le Royal oppure relax in una delle piscine: qui le due cose vanno di pari passo.

Raffles Hotel Le Royal *Phnom Penh, Cambodia*   79

While furnishing, the operators relied on nostalgia and preserved traditional elements such as free-standing bathtubes.

Bei der Einrichtung haben die Betreiber auf Nostalgie gesetzt und traditionelle Elemente, wie die freiste-hende Badewanne, erhalten.

Lors de l'aménagement, les propriétaires ont misé sur la nostalgie et les éléments traditionnels, comme la baignoire indépendante, conservée.

En cuanto al mobiliario, los gerentes se inclinaron por un estilo nostálgico y conservaron elementos tra-dicionales, como la bañera sin empotrar.

Nell'arredamento i gestori hanno puntato sulla nostalgia e hanno mantenuto elementi tradizionali, come la vasca da bagno coloniale.

Sofitel Metropole
Hanoi, Vietnam

Between Hoan Kiem Lake and the opera, the white colonial style building is an attraction. Opened 1901 as a grand hotel, it was expanded to 232 rooms in phases—most recently in 1996. The facility now nestles around a tropical garden with a pool. The charm of the 30's, when Somerset Maugham or Charlie Chaplin philosophized over their drinks in the hotel bar, still prevails. One of the highlights is the Le Beaulieu, reopened in 2003, with its "Cuisine de Soleil".

Zwischen dem Hoan Kiem See und der Oper ist der weiße Kolonialbau eine Sehenswürdigkeit. 1901 als Grandhotel eröffnet, wurde es in Etappen – zuletzt 1996 – auf 232 Zimmer erweitert. Heute schmiegt sich die Anlage um einen tropischen Garten mit Pool. Noch immer ist der Charme der 30er Jahre gegenwärtig, als in der Hotelbar Somerset Maugham oder Charlie Chaplin zu ihren Drinks philosophierten. Einer der Glanzpunkte ist das 2003 wieder eröffnete Le Beaulieu mit seiner „Cuisine de Soleil".

Entre le lac Hoan Kiem et l'opéra, la construction coloniale blanche est une curiosité. Le Grand hôtel a été ouvert en 1901, puis a été agrandi en plusieurs étapes – la dernière en 1996 – à 232 chambres. Aujourd'hui, le site comprend un jardin tropique avec piscine. Le charme des années 30 est toujours présent, lorsque Somerset Maugham ou Charlie Chaplin philosophaient devant leurs drinks au bar de l'hôtel. L'un des éléments somptueux est Le Beaulieu avec sa « Cuisine de Soleil », qui a ouvert de nouveau en 2003.

Entre el lago Hoan Kiem y la Ópera, la blanca construcción colonial es un monumento turístico. Inaugurado en 1901 como hotel de lujo, fue ampliado por etapas –la última en 1996– hasta alcanzar 232 habitaciones. Hoy el complejo se amolda a un jardín tropical con piscina. Todavía está presente el encanto de los años 30, cuando en el bar del hotel Somerset Maugham o Charlie Chaplin filosofaban mientras tomaban unos tragos. Una de las sensaciones es el restaurante Le Beaulieu, inaugurado nuevamente en 2003, avec sa "Cuisine de Soleil".

Tra il lago Hoan Kiem e il teatro dell'opera il bianco edificio coloniale è un luogo da vedere. Dall'apertura nel 1901 il grand hotel è stato poco per volta – ultimamente nel 1996 – ampliato fino a 232 camere. Oggi il complesso si modella intorno a un giardino tropicale con piscina. Ancora sempre attuale è il fascino degli anni Trenta, quando, nel bar dell'hotel, Somerset Maugham o Charlie Chaplin dissertavano davanti ai loro drink. Magnifico è Le Beaulieu riaperto nel 2003 con la sua "Cuisine de Soleil".

Whether in the pavilion winter garden, on the building façades, or on the interior walls, one meets white in connection with ornaments in French colonial style everywhere.

Ob im Wintergarten des Pavillons, an den Fassaden der Gebäude oder an den Innenwänden, überall trifft man auf Weiß in Verbindung mit Ornamenten im französischen Kolonialstil.

Que cela soit dans le jardin d'hiver du pavillon, sur les façades du bâtiment ou sur les murs intérieurs, on trouve partout du blanc en association avec des ornementations dans le style colonial français.

Sea en el invernadero del pabellón, en las fachadas del edificio o en las paredes interiores, el blanco está en todas partes en combinación con ornamentos de estilo colonial francés.

Nel giardino d'inverno del padiglione, sulle facciate degli edifici o sulle pareti interne, dappertutto il bianco si combina con gli ornamenti in stile coloniale francese.

With its six restaurants and bars, the hotel offers varied gastronomy. The Spices Garden Restaurant, with its authentic Vietnamese lunch buffet, is especially popular.

Mit seinen sechs Restaurants und Bars bietet das Hotel eine abwechslungsreiche Gastronomie. Besonders beliebt ist das Spices Garden Restaurant mit seinem authentischen vietnamesischen Mittagsbuffet.

Avec ses six restaurants et bars, l'hôtel offre une gastronomie variée. Le restaurant Spices Garden est particulièrement apprécié avec son buffet vietnamien authentique à midi.

Con sus seis restaurantes y bares, el hotel ofrece una gastronomía variada. Especialmente popular es el restaurante Spice Garden con su bufet del mediodía, auténticamente vietnamita.

Grazie ai suoi sei ristoranti e bar, l'hotel offre una gastronomia differenziata. Particolarmente amato è il ristorante Spices Garden con il suo buffet di mezzogiorno autenticamente vietnamita.

The 232 rooms including 31 suites are spread through the original building and the new Opera Wing. Whether in the inner courtyard or along the outer façade, the filigree roof projections protect one from the sometimes-vehement summer rains.

Die 232 Zimmer inklusive 31 Suiten verteilen sich auf das Originalgebäude und den neuen Opera Wing. Ob in den Innenhöfen oder entlang der Außenfassade, die filigranen Vordächer schützen vor den teilweise heftigen Sommerregen.

Les 232 chambres, y compris 31 suites, se répartissent dans le bâtiment d'origine et la nouvelle aile Opera Wing. Que ce soit dans les cours intérieures ou le long de la façade extérieure, les auvents filigranes protègent des averses d'été en partie violentes.

Las 232 habitaciones, incluyendo las 31 suites, están repartidas entre la construcción original y el ala nueva de la Ópera. Tanto en los patios interiores como a lo largo de la fachada, los aleros afiligranados son una protección contra las lluvias de verano, que a veces son muy fuertes.

Le 232 camere, incluse le 31 suite, si distribuiscono tra l'edificio originario e la nuova ala Opéra. Sia nei cortili interni, sia lungo la facciata esterna, le tettoie in filigrana riparano dalle intense, a volte violente, piogge estive.

Raffles Hotel

Singapore

The Raffles Hotel was established already in 1887. After several expansions, it has arrived at its present design in neo-renaissance style. The 103 suites are appointed with furniture from the hotels' period of origin, and two approximately hundred year old original tables invite one to sink the balls in the billiard room. Even an own museum that illustrates its history contributes to the atmosphere of the hotel temple, long since a legend.

Bereits 1887 wurde das Raffles Hotel gegründet, nach mehreren Erweiterungen erhielt es seine heutige Gestalt im Neorenaissance-Stil. Die 103 Suiten sind mit Möbeln aus der Entstehungszeit des Hotels eingerichtet, und im Billardraum laden zwei etwa hundert Jahre alte Originaltische zum Versenken der Kugeln ein. Zur Atmosphäre des längst zur Legende gewordenen Hoteltempels trägt auch ein eigenes Museum bei, das seine Geschichte veranschaulicht.

Le Raffles Hotel a été créé dès 1887, il obtint sa forme actuelle en style néorenaissance après plusieurs agrandissements. Les 103 suites sont aménagées avec des meubles datant de l'époque de la création de l'hôtel, et deux tables d'origine vieilles d'environ cent ans invitent dans la salle de billard à faire disparaître les boules. Un musée de l'hôtel retraçant son histoire contribue à l'ambiance du temple-hôtel entré depuis longtemps dans la légende.

El Raffles Hotel fue fundado ya en 1887; tras muchas ampliaciones alcanzó su aspecto actual de estilo neorrenacentista. Las 103 suites están decoradas con muebles de la época de su inauguración y en el salón de billar dos mesas originales de aproximadamente 100 años de antigüedad invitan al juego. Al ambiente de este hotel-templo, convertido en leyenda desde hace ya tiempo, contribuye un museo propio que ilustra su historia.

Il Raffles Hotel fu fondato già nel 1887; dopo diversi ampliamenti ha ricevuto la forma odierna in stile neorinascimentale. Le 103 suite sono arredate con mobili dell'epoca in cui sorse l'hotel, e nella sala da biliardo due originali tavoli di quasi cento anni invitano a buttare le bilie in buca. All'atmosfera da hotel, da molto tempo ormai una leggenda, contribuisce anche un museo proprio, che ne illustra la storia.

In the midst of the booming Singapore skyscraper metropolis, The Raffles remains true to its traditions. It was declared a National Monument in 1987.

Inmitten der boomenden Hochhausmetropole Singapur bleibt The Raffles seinen Traditionen treu. 1987 wurde es zum nationalen Monument erklärt.

Situé au centre de Singapour, la métropole bouillonnante des gratte-ciels, The Raffles reste fidèle à ses traditions. Il a été nommé en 1987 National Monument.

En medio de esta próspera metrópoli de rascacielos, The Raffles sigue fiel a sus tradiciones. En 1987 fue declarado Monumento Nacional.

Nel centro di Singapore, metropoli di grattacieli in pieno boom, The Raffles resta fedele alle sue tradizioni. Nel 1987 è stato dichiarato National Monument.

Rhapsody in white: the lobby, twelve restaurants and five bars radiate bright generosity.

Rhapsodie in Weiß: Die Lobby, zwölf Restaurants und fünf Bars verbreiten helle Großzügigkeit.

Rapsodie en blanc : le hall, douze restaurants et cinq bars répandent une grande étendue claire.

Rapsodia en blanco: El vestíbulo, doce restaurantes y cinco bares irradian una luminosa amplitud.

Rapsodia in bianco: l'ingresso, dodici ristoranti e cinque bar diffondono un senso di spaziosità luminosa.

The rooms, *partially four meters high, testify to the spaciousness of the hotel buildings at the end of the 19th century.*

Die teilweise *über vier Meter hohen Räume zeugen von der Großzügigkeit von Hotelbauten am Ende des 19. Jahrhunderts.*

Les pièces, *en partie d'une hauteur de plus de quatre mètres, sont les témoins de la grandeur des bâtiments de l'hôtel à la fin du 19ème siècle.*

Los salones, *en parte con techos de más de cuatro metros de altura, dan testimonio de la amplitud de las construcciones hoteleras de finales del siglo XIX.*

Le camere *a volte alte più di quattro metri testimoniano della spaziosità degli edifici alberghieri alla fine del XIX secolo.*

The Fullerton

Singapore

In 1928, the Fullerton was erected in neoclassicist style and accommodated the main post office, the chamber of commerce and the stock exchange one after the other before finally being opened as one of the most beautiful new hotels in Singapore in 2001. Situated between the Singapore River and the Marina Bay, over half of the rooms offer a multifarious view of the water and skyline. On top of that, from here almost the entire city center can be reached by foot.

1928 wurde das Fullerton im neoklassizistischen Stil errichtet und beherbergte nacheinander das Hauptpostamt, die Handelskammer und die Börse, bevor es 2001 schließlich als eines der schönsten neuen Hotels in Singapur eröffnet wurde. Zwischen dem Singapur River und der Marina-Bucht gelegen, bieten über die Hälfte der Räume eine abwechslungsreiche Aussicht auf Wasser und Skyline. Zudem ist von hier aus nahezu das gesamte Stadtzentrum zu Fuß erreichbar.

Le Fullerton a été fondé en 1928 dans le style néoclassique et hébergea l'un après l'autre la poste principale, la chambre du commerce et la bourse, avant que l'un des plus beaux hôtels récents de Singapour ne soit finalement ouvert en 2001. Situées entre la Singapur River et la baie de Marina, plus de la moitié des pièces offrent une vue variée sur l'eau et les gratte-ciels. De plus, d'ici, quasiment la totalité du centre-ville est accessible à pied.

El Fullerton fue construido en 1928 en estilo neoclásico y albergó sucesivamente la oficina de correos, la cámara de comercio y la bolsa, antes de ser inaugurado en 2001 como uno de los más hermosos hoteles de Singapur. Ubicado entre el río Singapur y Marina Bay, más de la mitad de las habitaciones ofrecen una variada vista hacia el río y el skyline de la ciudad. Además, se puede ir andando a casi todas las zonas del centro.

Il Fullerton fu eretto nel 1928 in stile neoclassico e ha ospitato una dopo l'altra la Posta Centrale, la Camera di Commercio e la Borsa, prima di venire infine riaperto nel 2001 come uno dei più belli e nuovi hotel di Singapore. Situato tra il Singapur River e la baia Marina, più della metà delle camere offre una vista variata sull'acqua e sullo skyline. Inoltre di qui è raggiungibile a piedi quasi tutto il centro della città.

Modern use of a historic building: the glazed winter garden in the Governor's Suite fits in with the high colonnades.

Moderne Nutzung für ein historisches Gebäude: Unauffällig fügt sich der verglaste Wintergarten der Governor's Suite unter die hohen Kolonnaden.

Utilisation moderne pour un bâtiment historique : le jardin d'hiver vitré de la suite Governor s'intègre discrètement sous les hautes colonnades.

Una utilización moderna para un edificio histórico: Discretamente se integra el invernadero de cristal a la suite Governor bajo las altas columnas.

Destinazione moderna di un edificio storico: le vetrate del giardino d'inverno si inseriscono con discrezione alla Governor's suite sotto gli alti colonnati.

Part of the hotel rooms is oriented inwards to the imposing glass covered atrium.

Ein Teil der Hotelzimmer orientiert sich nach innen zu dem imposanten glasüberdeckten Atrium.

Une partie des chambres de l'hôtel est orientée vers l'intérieur vers l'imposant atrium recouvert de verre.

Parte de las habitaciones se dirigen hacia el interior, hacia el imponente atrio cubierto con techo de cristal.

Una parte delle camere dell'hotel dà all'interno verso l'imponente atrio con copertura in vetro.

The water location, now very picturesque, used to have concrete advantages when the building housed the post office: letters and packages were distributed by boat.

Die Lage am Wasser, heute sehr malerisch, hatte früher, als das Gebäude noch die Post beherbergte, handfeste Vorteile: Briefe und Pakete wurden mit dem Boot verteilt.

Sa situation au bord de l'eau, aujourd'hui très pittoresque, comportait autrefois, lorsque le bâtiment hébergeait la poste, de grands avantages : les lettres et les colis étaient distribuées par bateau.

La situación a orillas del río, actualmente tan pintoresca, tenía, en la época en que albergaba la oficina de correos, una ventaja contundente: Las cartas y los paquetes se repartían con el bote.

La posizione sull'acqua, oggi molto pittoresca, era un tempo, quando l'edificio ospitava ancora la Posta, di grande vantaggio: lettere e pacchetti venivano distribuiti con la barca.

The Sentosa Resort & Spa
Singapore

The Sentosa Resort & Spa of the Beaufort Hotels awaits guests who want to escape the hectic city life in Singapore. The small island at the door of the city is only a 10-minute drive from the center. 210 rooms and suites are spread over several flat buildings in nostalgic colonial style, which duck under tropical trees. Four garden villas with two bedrooms each even have their own pool. One highlight is the recently opened Spa Botanica, one of the most beautiful in Asia.

Auf Gäste, die in Singapur der Hektik der Stadt entfliehen möchten, ohne abseits zu wohnen, wartet The Sentosa Resort & Spa der Beaufort Hotels. Die kleine Insel vor der Stadt ist nur zehn Autominuten vom Zentrum entfernt. 210 Zimmer und Suiten verteilen sich auf mehrere flache Bauten im nostalgischen Kolonialstil, die sich unter tropische Bäume ducken. Vier Gartenvillen mit jeweils zwei Schlafzimmern verfügen gar über einen eigenen Pool. Ein Highlight ist das kürzlich eröffnete Spa Botanica, eines der schönsten in Asien.

The Sentosa Resort & Spa des hôtels Beaufort attend les hôtes qui souhaitent fuir à Singapour le stress de la ville sans habiter à l'extérieur. La petite île précédant la ville ne se trouve qu'à dix minutes en voiture du centre. 210 chambres et suites sont réparties sur plusieurs bâtiments plats dans le style colonial nostalgique et se penchent sous les arbres tropicaux. Quatre villas de jardin avec chacune deux chambres à coucher disposent même de leur propre piscine. Un élément splendide est le Spa Botanica ouvert récemment, l'un des plus beaux en Asie.

A los huéspedes que quieren huir del trajín de la ciudad en Singapur, sin tener que alojarse en las afueras, les espera el The Sentosa Resort & Spa de la cadena de hoteles Beaufort. La pequeña isla queda a sólo 10 minutos en coche del centro de la ciudad. 210 habitaciones y suites se distribuyen en varias construcciones planas de nostálgico estilo colonial, ocultas bajo árboles tropicales. Cuatro chalés en el jardín, cada uno con dos habitaciones, disponen incluso de piscina propia. Una de las atracciones más destacadas es el Spa Botanica recientemente inaugurado, uno de los más bellos de Asia.

The Sentosa Resort & Spa degli hoteles Beaufort attende gli ospiti che a Singapore desiderano sfuggire alla frenesia della città, senza alloggiare distante. La piccola isola di fronte alla città è lontana solo dieci minuti di macchina dal centro. Le 210 camere e suite si distribuiscono su diverse costruzioni basse in nostalgico stile coloniale, poste sotto agli alberi tropicali. Quattro villini con giardino, ognuno con due camere da letto, dispongono persino di una piscina propria. Il pezzo forte è la Spa Botanica aperta recentemente, una delle più belle dell'Asia.

Kerry Hill Architects have counted on clear lines and the reduced use of decorative elements here also. The transitions between architecture and nature, between inside and outside, is constantly fluid.

Kerry Hill Architects haben auch hier auf klare Linien und den reduzierten Einsatz dekorativer Elemente gesetzt. Die Übergänge zwischen Architektur und Natur, zwischen innen und außen sind stets fließend.

Ici également, Kerry Hill Architects a misé sur des lignes claires et l'utilisation limitée d'éléments décoratifs. Les transitions entre architecture et nature, entre l'intérieur et l'extérieur, sont toujours floues.

La firma Kerry Hill Architects se decidió aquí también por líneas claras y un reducido uso de elementos decorativos. La transición entre arquitectura y naturaleza, entre interior y exterior constantemente fluye.

Lo studio Kerry Hill Architects ha puntato anche qui su linee chiare e sull'impiego limitato di elementi decorativi. Le frontiere tra architettura e natura, tra dentro e fuori sono sempre fluide.

Asian minimalism meets a tropical landscape. Whether in the new Spa Botanica, in the guest rooms, or in one of the four villas with own pool.

Asiatischer Minimalismus trifft hier auf eine tropische Landschaft. Sei dies im neuen Spa Botanica, in den Gästezimmern oder in einer der vier Villen mit eigenem Pool.

Le minimalisme asiatique affronte ici un paysage tropique. Que ce soit dans le nouveau Spa Botanica, dans les chambres des hôtes ou dans l'une des quatre villas avec piscine.

El minimalismo asiático se reúne aquí con el paisaje tropical. Sea en el nuevo Spa Botanica, en las habitaciones o en uno de los cuatro chalés con piscina propia.

Il minimalismo asiatico qui si incontra con un paesaggio tropicale: nella nuova Spa Botanica, nelle camere per gli ospiti o in una dei quattro villini con piscina propria.

The Dharmawangsa

Jakarta, Indonesia

Quiet and space are pure luxury in Jakarta, a city of millions. In one of the posh residential areas before the city gates, one finds what one seeks: an elegant hotel, furnished with princely four-poster beds made from rosewood, antique inlaid-work furniture, and silk pillows is hidden in a snug garden. The rooms and penthouse suites adapt the Java, Bali, East-Indonesian and South-Sumatra styles. And if one is drawn to the city: the Kemag nightclub district is not far off.

Ruhe und Platz sind wahrer Luxus in der Millionenmetropole Jakarta. In einem vornehmen Villenviertel vor den Toren der Metropole findet man das Gesuchte: Hier versteckt sich in einem lauschigen Garten ein elegantes Hotel, ausgestattet mit fürstlichen Himmelbetten aus Rosenholz, antikem Intarsien-Mobiliar und Seidenkissen. Die Zimmer und Penthouse-Suiten sind den Stilen der Regionen Java, Bali, Ost-Indonesien und Süd-Sumatra nachempfunden. Und wen es doch in die Stadt zieht: das Amüsierviertel Kemag ist nicht weit.

Le clame et la place sont un réel luxe à Jakarta, métropole comptant plusieurs millions d'habitants. Dans un quartier de villas distingué devant les portes de la métropole, on trouve ce que l'on cherchait : un élégant hôtel se cache ici dans un jardin où se sent vraiment bien, aménagé avec des lits à baldaquin princiers en bois de rose, du mobilier antique en marqueterie et des coussins en soie. Les chambres et suites penthouse sont inspirées des styles des régions de Java, de Bali, d'Indonésie de l'Est et du Sumatra du Sud. Et si le besoin d'aller en ville se fait quand même sentir : le quartier chaud Kemag n'est pas loin.

Tranquilidad y espacio son verdaderos lujos en una metrópoli tan densamente poblada como Jakarta. En un elegante barrio residencial a las puertas de la ciudad se encuentra lo buscado: Aquí se esconde en medio de un acogedor jardín un elegante hotel, dotado de fantásticas camas con dosel hechas de palo de rosa, antiguo mobiliario con incrustaciones y cojines de seda. Las habitaciones y las suites del penthouse están decoradas en los estilos de las regiones de Java, Bali, Indonesia oriental y el Sur de Sumatra. Y si de todas formas la ciudad llama: La zona de diversión Kemag no se encuentra muy lejos.

Tranquillità e spazio nella grande metropoli di Giacarta sono un vero lusso. In un quartiere residenziale signorile ed esclusivo alle porte della metropoli si trova quello che si cerca: qui in un giardino appartato si nasconde un hotel elegante, arredato con principeschi letti a baldacchino in legno di rosa, antica mobilia intarsiata e cuscini di seta. Le camere e i penthouse suite si rifanno agli stili di Giava, di Bali, dell'Indonesia Orientale e di Sumatra del sud. Ma chi si sente attratto dalla città? Il quartiere dei locali notturni, Kemag, non è lontano.

Contrasts: traditional Sumatra architecture in the top class Sriwijaya restaurant, modern minimalism in the Japanese The Sekitei or boutique style in the suites.

Gegensätze: Traditionelle Sumatra-Architektur im Nobelrestaurant Sriwijaya, moderner Minimalismus im japanischen The Sekitei oder Boutiquestil in den Suiten.

Contraires : une architecture Sumatra traditionnelle dans le restaurant chic Sriwijaya, le minimalisme moderne dans The Sekitei japonais ou le style boutique dans les suites.

Contrastes: Arquitectura tradicional de Sumatra en el elegante restaurante Sriwijaya, minimalismo moderno en el The Sekitei japonés o estilo boutique en las suites.

Contrasti: l'architettura tradizionale di Sumatra nel lussuoso ristorante Sriwijaya, il minimalismo moderno nel giapponese The Sekitei o lo stile esclusivo nelle suite.

By intelligently arranging the rooms, a private residential atmosphere arises everywhere, for instance in the library or Cigar Bar. Even roaming the hallways is an optical treat.

Durch intelligent angeordnete Räumlichkeiten entsteht überall private Wohnatmosphäre, wie etwa in der Bibliothek oder in der Cigar Bar. Selbst das Wandeln in den Fluren ist ein optischer Genuss.

On ressent partout une atmosphère privée grâce à des pièces ordonnées avec intelligence, comme par exemple dans la bibliothèque ou le Cigar Bar. Même se déplacer dans les couloirs est un plaisir pour les yeux.

A través de espacios inteligentemente organizados se logra la sensación de tener ambientes privados en todas partes, como por ejemplo, en la biblioteca o en el bar Cigar. Incluso andar por los pasillos se convierte en un placer visual.

Grazie agli spazi disposti con intelligenza si crea ovunque un'atmosfera da abitazione privata, come per esempio nella biblioteca e nel Cigar Bar. Persino passeggiare nei corridoi è un piacere degli occhi.

Park and pool *as well as the largest of the suites with their exceedingly generous bathrooms impart the guests with the feeling of being on an estate.*

Park und Pool *sowie die größeren unter den Suiten mit ihren überaus geräumigen Badezimmern vermitteln den Gästen das Gefühl, sich auf einem Landgut zu befinden.*

Le parc et la piscine, *ainsi que les plus grandes des suites avec leurs salles de bains extrêmement spacieuses, donnent aux hôtes la sensation de se trouver dans un domaine.*

El parque y la piscina, *así como las suites más grandes con sus amplísimos baños, proporcionan al huésped la sensación de estar en una hacienda.*

Parco e piscina, *ma anche le suite più grandi con i loro bagni estremamente spaziosi trasmettono agli ospiti la sensazione di trovarsi in una tenuta.*

Amandari

Bali, Indonesia

Near the artists' colony Ubud, amongst rice terraces, the first Amanresort in Bali fits smoothly into the scenery. Roomy villas made from volcanic rock lie within tropical vegetation. One bathes under the sky, surrounded by bamboo and ferns. As in a Bali village, spaces all around invite to linger. Jungle paths lead to a restaurant and saltwater pool. One experiences impressive moments when the wind carries the melodies of the Gamelan players over the fields and the herons climb.

Nahe der Künstlerkolonie Ubud, inmitten von Reisterrassen, fügt sich das erste Amanresort auf Bali harmonisch in die grüne Landschaft. Geräumige Villen aus Vulkangestein liegen inmitten tropischer Vegetation. Gebadet wird unter freiem Himmel, umgeben von Bambus und Farn. Wie in einem balinesischen Dorf laden überall Plätze zum Verweilen ein. Dschungelpfade führen zu Restaurant und Salzwasserpool. Stimmungsvolle Momente lassen sich erleben, wenn der Wind die Melodien der Gamelan-Spieler über die Felder trägt und Reiher aufsteigen.

Près de la colonie des artistes Ubud, au milieu des terrasses de riz, le premier hôtel de Amanresort à Bali s'intègre harmonieusement dans le paysage vert. Des villas spacieuses en roche volcanique se trouvent au milieu de la végétation tropicale. On se baigne en plein air, entouré de bambous et de fougères. Comme dans un village balinais, on trouve partout des endroits invitant au repos. Les sentiers dans la jungle mènent au restaurant et à la piscine d'eau salée. On peut vivre des instants évocateurs lorsque le vent emporte dans les champs les mélodies des joueurs de gamelan et que les hérons s'envolent.

Cerca de la colonia de artistas Ubud, en medio de terrazas de arroz, se integra el primer Amanresort en el verde paisaje. Espaciosos chalés hechos de roca volcánica se encuentran en medio de una vegetación trópical. El baño se toma al aire libre, en medio de cañas de bambú y helechos. Igual que en un pueblo balinés, en todas partes hay lugares que invitan a quedarse. Senderos en la selva conducen al restaurante y a la piscina de agua salada. Se viven momentos maravillosos cuando el viento esparce las melodías de los músicos gamelan sobre los campos y las garzas alzan el vuelo.

Vicino a Ubud, la colonia di artisti, in mezzo alle terrazze di riso, si inserisce armonicamente nel verde paesaggio il primo Amanresort nel Bali. Ville spaziose di pietra vulcanica si trovano nel mezzo della vegetazione tropicale. Si fa il bagno all'aperto, circondati da bambù e da felci. Come in un villaggio balinese dappertutto ci sono posti che invitano a soffermarsi. Sentieri nella giungla conducono a un ristorante e alla piscina di acqua salata. Si vivono momenti molto suggestivi quando il vento porta sui campi le melodie dei suonatori di gamelan e gli aironi si alzano in volo.

There are still cozy seats and couchettes under the pool, after that the rice terraces start.

Unterhalb des Pools gibt es noch lauschige Sitz- und Liegeplätze, danach beginnen die Reisterrassen.

Sous la piscine se trouvent encore de confortables sièges et chaises longues, puis les terrasses de riz commencent.

Más abajo de la piscina hay cómodos lugares para sentarse y tumbarse, después comienzan las terrazas de arroz.

Sotto la piscina ci sono ancora luoghi appartati dove sedersi o stare sdraiati, poi iniziano le terrazze di riso.

The tropical surroundings *define the airy and open architecture of the living and bedrooms.*

Die tropische Umgebung *bestimmt die luftige und offene Architektur der Wohn- und Schlafräume.*

L'environnement tropique *détermine l'architecture aérée et ouverte des pièces de séjour et des chambres à coucher.*

El entorno tropical *determina la arquitectura abierta, con mucha ventilación, de los salones y habitaciones.*

L'ambiente tropicale *influenza l'architettura ariosa e aperta delle sale e delle camere da letto.*

Amandari *Bali, Indonesia* 115

Four Seasons Resort Bali at Sayan

Bali, Indonesia

This hotel on the edge of a plateau with a breathtaking view built by John Heah sits like a huge UFO. The airy villas are spread around the wide rice terrace steps. One enters via a roof garden with a sun deck and lotus pond. Under the rooms in the main building and the villa lies the pool, following the contours of the Ayung River. A Yoga session on one of the wooden terraces with a panoramic view belongs to the highlights.

Wie ein riesiges Ufo liegt dieses von John Heah erbaute Hotel am Rande eines Hochplateaus mit atemberaubender Aussicht. Die luftigen Villen verteilen sich auf die breiten Stufen der Reiserrassen. Man betritt sie über einen Dachgarten mit Sonnendeck und Lotus-Teich. Unterhalb der Zimmer im Hauptgebäude und der Villen liegt der Pool, der den Konturen des Ayung-Flusses folgt. Zu den Höhepunkten gehört eine Yogastunde auf einer der Holzterrassen mit Panoramablick.

Tel un OVNI géant, cet l'hôtel a été construit par John Heah au bord du haut plateau avec une vue à en couper le souffle. Les villas aérées sont réparties sur les larges marches des terrasses de riz. On y accède par un jardin sur le toit avec pont supérieur et étang de lotus. Sous les chambres se trouvant dans le bâtiment principal et sous les villas se trouve la piscine qui suit les contours du fleuve Ayung. Une heure de yoga sur l'une des terrasses en bois avec vue panoramique fait partie des grands moments à vivre.

Igual que un inmenso platillo volador se encuentra el hotel construido por John Heah al borde de una meseta, con una vista impresionante. Los ventilados chalés se distribuyen en los amplios escalones de las terrazas de arroz. Se entra por una azotea jardín con cubierta para tomar el sol y estanque de lotos. Más abajo de las habitaciones del edificio principal y de los chalés se encuentra la piscina, que sigue el contorno del río Ayung. Una de las atracciones destacadas es una hora de yoga en alguna de las terrazas de madera con vista panorámica.

Come un gigantesco Ufo, questo hotel costruito da John Heah è situato ai margini di un altopiano con una vista mozzafiato. Gli ariosi villini si distribuiscono sugli ampi gradoni delle terrazze di riso. Vi si accede da un giardino pensile con solarium e stagno con fiori di loto. Sotto le camere dell'edificio principale e i villini si trova la piscina, che segue i contorni del fiume Ayung. Uno dei momenti culminati è l'ora di yoga su una delle terrazze di legno con vista panoramica.

Unique architecture and top service are combined here to a mixture with a magnetic attraction. Especially if one glances from the open bar over the rice fields into the jungle.

Einzigartige Architektur und Top-Service verbinden sich hier zu einer Mischung mit magnetischer Anziehungskraft. Besonders, wenn man von der offenen Bar über die Reisfelder in den Dschungel blickt.

Architecture unique et service de première classe s'allient ici en un mélange avec une force d'attraction magnétique. Surtout lorsque l'on admire, du bar ouvert, la jungle par-dessus les champs de riz.

Aquí se unen una arquitectura exclusiva y un servicio de primera, dando lugar a una combinación irresistible. En especial, cuando se está en el bar abierto y se ve la selva detrás de los campos de arroz.

Architettura unica e servizio eccellente si mescolano qui con una forza di attrazione magnetica; in particolare quando dal bar aperto sui campi di riso si volge lo sguardo alla giungla.

Water is the dominant theme in the spa and guests' villas as well as in the public areas. There is even a lotus blossom pond situated on the building roof.

In den Spa- und Gästevillen sowie in den öffentlichen Räumen ist Wasser das dominante Thema. Auf dem Dach des Gebäudes ist sogar ein Lotusblütenteich angelegt.

Dans les villas spa et les villas pour hôtes ainsi que dans les pièces publiques, l'eau est le thème dominant. Sur le toit du bâtiment, un étang de fleurs de lotus a même été aménagé.

En el spa y en los chalés para huéspedes, así como en los salones comunales, el agua es elemento determinante. Incluso sobre el tejado se encuentra un estanque de lotos.

Sia nei villini degli ospiti e delle terme sia negli spazi comuni, l'acqua è il tema dominante. Sul tetto dell'edificio è stato persino allestito uno stagno con fiori di loto.

Four Seasons Resort Bali at Sayan *Bali, Indonesia* 119

The stairway leads from the lobby with its spectacular open-air bar into the restaurant underneath.

Das Treppenhaus führt von der Lobby mit seiner spektakulären Open-Air-Bar in das darunter liegende Restaurant.

L'escalier nous mène du hall, avec son bar open-air spectaculaire, au restaurant situé en dessous.

Por la escalera del vestíbulo, con su espectacular bar al aire libre, se baja al restaurante.

La scala conduce dall'ingresso, con il suo spettacolare bar all'aperto, al sottostante ristorante.

Uma Ubud

Bali, Indonesia

Along with the Metropolitan Hotel and the Como Resort, Christina Ong created a further brand for her group with Uma, realizing the first resorts in Bhutan and on Bali. They combine the rustic transformation of contemporary design with a practical, ethical, and aesthetic awareness for indigenous cultures. In Bahasa, the Indonesian national language, Uma means "living house". The stay in one of the 24 Terrace or Garden Rooms or one of the pool suites promises lively dwelling.

Neben den Metropolitan Hotels und den Como Resorts hat Christina Ong für ihre Gruppe mit Uma eine weitere Marke kreiert und in Bhutan sowie auf Bali erste Resorts verwirklicht. Sie vereint die rustikalere Umsetzung zeitgenössischen Designs mit einem praktikablen, ethischen und ästhetischen Bewusstsein für einheimische Kulturen. In Bahasa, der indonesischen Landessprache, bedeutet Uma „lebendiges Haus". Lebendiges Wohnen verspricht der Aufenthalt in einer der 24 Terrace oder Garden Rooms bzw. einer der Pool Suiten.

Parallèlement à l'hôtel Metropolitan et aux Como Resorts, Christina Ong a créé avec Uma pour son groupe une autre marque et réalisé les premiers hôtels de tourisme à Bhutan ainsi qu'à Bali. Elle réunit la concrétisation la plus rustique de designs contemporains avec une connaissance praticable, éthique et esthétique pour les cultures locales. En Bahasa, la langue nationale indonésienne, Uma signifie « maison vivante ». Le séjour dans l'un des 24 Terrace ou Garden Rooms, voire l'une des suites avec piscine, promet un logement vivant.

Además de Metropolitan Hotels y Como Resorts Christina Ong ha creado para su grupo una nueva marca con el Uma y ha hecho realidad los primeros resorts en Bután y en Bali. Ella reúne la implementación rustical del diseño contemporáneo con una conciencia factible, ética y estética de las culturas nativas. En bahasa, el idioma indonesio, Uma significa "casa viva". Vivir lleno de vida es lo que ofrece la estadía en una de las 24 habitaciones en las terrazas o en el jardín, o bien en una de las suites de la piscina.

Accanto ai Metropolitan Hotel e ai Como Resort, Christina Ong ha con Uma creato un'ulteriore marca per il suo gruppo e tanto nel Bhutan come a Bali ha realizzato i primi resort. Unisce le applicazioni rustiche del design contemporaneo a una consapevolezza per le culture locali praticabile, etica ed estetica. In bahasa indonesia, la lingua nazionale indonesiana, uma significa "casa viva". Un abitare pieno di vita, infatti, viene promesso dal soggiorno in una delle 24 camere con terrazza o giardino oppure in una delle suite con piscina.

Penetrating deeply into the Bali culture and tropical nature in the frame of modern architecture: that is what is promised by the newest luxury resort in Ubud.

Im Rahmen moderner Architektur tief eindringen in die balinesische Kultur und die tropische Natur: Dies verspricht das neueste Luxusresort in Ubud.

Entrer dans la culture balinaise et la nature tropicale dans un cadre d'architecture moderne : c'est ce que promet l'hôtel de tourisme de luxe le plus récent à Ubud.

Con una arquitectura moderna penetrar profundamente en la cultura balinesa y en la naturaleza tropical. Esto es lo que promete el más reciente resort de lujo en Ubud.

Nella cornice di un'architettura moderna, entrare nel profondo della cultura balinese e della natura tropicale: questo promette il nuovissimo resort di lusso a Ubud.

Contrasts: *nice quiet corners, high-tech with plasma displays and DVD players and open-air bathrooms.*

Gegensätze: *Lauschige Plätze, High-Tech mit Plasmabildschirmen und DVD Playern sowie Freiluft-Badezimmer.*

Contraires : *lieux confortables, haute technologie avec écrans plasma et lecteurs DVD ainsi que salles de bains en pleine air.*

Contrastes: *Lugares acogedores, alta tecnología con pantallas plasma y videodisco digital, así como baños al aire libre.*

Contrasti: *luoghi appartati, high tech con schermo al plasma e DVD, nonché stanze da bagno aperte.*

The Peninsula Palace

Beijing, China

An American travel magazine recently ennobled the Peninsula Palace to the best hotel in China. Its 478 rooms and 52 suites offer several technical specialties, such as a television in the bathroom and a thermostat next to the door that states the outside temperature and humidity. The suites in the upper floors stretch over two floors. Hungry guests can choose between two restaurants, among which the Huang Ting awaits with Cantonese cuisine.

Ein amerikanisches Reisemagazin adelte den Peninsula Palace unlängst zum besten Hotel Chinas. Seine 478 Zimmer und 52 Suiten bieten einige technische Besonderheiten, etwa einen Fernseher im Badezimmer oder ein Thermostat neben der Tür, das Außentemperatur und Luftfeuchtigkeit angibt. Die Suiten in den oberen Geschossen erstrecken sich über zwei Stockwerke. Hungrige Gäste haben die Wahl zwischen zwei Restaurants, von denen das Huang Ting mit kantonesischer Küche aufwartet.

Un magazine de voyage américain a récemment fait honneur au Peninsula Palace en le nommant meilleur hôtel de Chine. Ses 478 chambres et 52 suites offrent certaines particularités techniques, par exemple un téléviseur dans la salle de bains ou un thermostat près de la porte qui indique la température extérieure et l'humidité dans l'air. Les suites des étages supérieurs s'étendent sur deux étages. Les hôtes affamés ont le choix entre deux restaurants, dont le Huang Ting qui propose de la cuisine cantonaise.

Una revista de turismo estadounidense catalogó recientemente al Peninsula Palace como el mejor hotel de China. Sus 478 habitaciones y 52 suites ofrecen algunas especialidades técnicas, como un televisor en el baño o un termostato al lado de la puerta que indica la temperatura exterior y la humedad. Las suites en los pisos superiores son dúplex. El huésped hambriento puede elegir entre dos restaurantes, uno de los cuales, el Huang Ting, ofrece cocina cantonesa.

Una rivista di viaggi americana di recente ha conferito al Peninsula Palace il titolo di migliore hotel della Cina. Le sue 478 stanze e 52 suite offrono alcune singolarità tecniche, per esempio un televisore nella stanza da bagno o, accanto alla porta, un termostato che indica la temperatura esterna e l'umidità dell'aria. Le suite superiori si estendono su due piani. Gli ospiti che hanno fame possono scegliere fra due ristoranti, dei quali lo Huang Ting serve cucina cantonese.

Modern furnishings dominate in the duplex suites; in the Jing Restaurant, transparent curtains screen the tables from each other.

In den Duplex-Suiten herrscht eine moderne Einrichtung vor, im Restaurant Jing schirmen transparente Vorhänge die Tische voneinander ab.

Dans les suites Duplex domine un aménagement moderne, des rideaux transparents séparent les tables l'une des autres dans le restaurant Jing.

En las suites dúplex predomina una decoración moderna, en el restaurante Jing las mesas se separan unas de otras por cortinas transparentes.

Nelle duplex suite domina un arredamento moderno, nel ristorante Jing tende trasparenti isolano i tavoli gli uni dagli altri.

Creamy hues and much wood characterize the Club Lounge; marble the bath of the Beijing suites.

Beige-Töne und viel Holz prägen die Club Lounge, Marmor das Bad der Beijing-Suiten.

Des tons crème et beaucoup de bois caractérisent la Club Lounge, et du marbre pour la salle de bains des suites Beijing.

Tonos cremosos y mucha madera caracterizan el Club Lounge; y mármol, el baño de las suites Beijing.

Tonalità crema e molto legno caratterizzano il Club Lounge, marmo invece per il bagno delle suite Pechino.

Escalators and a fountain lend the lobby a trace of shopping center flair. In the bar, things are more leisurely.

Rolltreppen und ein Brunnen geben der Lobby einen Hauch von Shopping-Center-Flair. In der Bar geht es gemütlicher zu.

Des escaliers roulants et une fontaine donnent au hall un soupçon de flair de shopping-center. Dans le bar, l'ambiance est plus à l'agréable.

Escaleras mecánicas y una fuente le dan al vestíbulo el encanto de un centro comercial. El bar es muy acogedor.

Scale mobili e una fontana danno all'ingresso un tocco di flair da shopping center. Il bar ha un ambiente più accogliente.

Grand Hyatt Shanghai
Shanghai, China

The Grand Hyatt Shanghai describes itself as the highest hotel in the world as it occupies the 53rd to 87th floors in the Jin Mao Tower. An additional superlative: it supposedly has the largest rooms in the city. The 555 accommodations offer a view of the Huang Pu River or the city and offer a special feature in the bathrooms: a heated mirror in the shower always ensures a clear view. The hotel's location in the financial district Pudong makes it an ideal domicile for business travelers.

Als höchstes Hotel der Welt bezeichnet sich das Grand Hyatt Shanghai, denn es nimmt das 53. bis 87. Stockwerk des Jin Mao Towers ein. Eine weitere Superlative: Es soll über die größten Zimmer der Stadt verfügen. Die 555 Unterkünfte bieten einen Blick über den Fluss Huang Pu oder die Stadt und warten mit einer Besonderheit im Badezimmer auf: Ein beheizter Spiegel in der Dusche sorgt stets für einen klaren Blick. Die Lage des Hotels im Finanzbezirk Pudong ist ideal als Domizil für Geschäftsreisende.

Le Grand Hyatt Shanghai se dit l'hôtel le plus haut du monde car il occupe les étages 53 à 87 de la Jin Mao Tower. Un autre plus : il paraît qu'il dispose des plus grandes chambres de la ville. Les 555 logements ont vue sur le fleuve Huang Pu ou la ville et comportent une particularité dans la salle de bains : un miroir chauffé dans la douche permet que la vue soit toujours nette. La situation de l'hôtel dans le quartier des banques Pudong est idéale comme domicile pour les voyages d'affaires.

El Grand Hyatt Shanghai se considera el hotel más alto del mundo pues ocupa los pisos 53 al 87 de la torre Jin Mao. Un superlativo más: Se dice que tiene las habitaciones más grandes de la ciudad. Las 555 habitaciones tienen vista del río Huang Pu o de la ciudad y ofrecen algo especial en el baño: Un espejo con calefacción en la ducha proporciona siempre una imagen despejada. La ubicación en el centro financiero Pudong lo hace el domicilio ideal para hombres y mujeres en viaje de negocios.

Il più alto hotel del mondo. Così si definisce il Grand Hyatt Shanghai, che occupa i piani tra il 53 e 87 della Jin Mao Tower. Ancora un superlativo: si dice che disponga delle più grandi camere della città. Le 555 sistemazioni offrono una vista sul fiume Huang Pu o sulla città e presentano una particolarità nel bagno: uno specchio riscaldato nella doccia fa sì che ci si possa sempre vedere nitidamente. La posizione dell'hotel nel quartiere delle banche Pudong lo rende il domicilio ideale per chi viaggia per affari.

A spectacular atrium, reaching across 33 floors, makes the guest rooms accessible.

Ein spektakuläres Atrium, *das über 33 Geschosse reicht, erschließt die Gästezimmer.*

Un atrium spectaculaire *qui s'étend sur 33 étages révèle les chambres des hôtes.*

Un Vestíbulo espectacular *alcanzando la altura de 33 pisos da acceso a las habitaciones.*

Un atrio spettacolare, *che si estende su 33 piani, si apre sulle camere per i clienti.*

The public area's floor space is especially extravagantly designed.

Die Bodenflächen der öffentlichen Räume sind besonders aufwändig gestaltet.

Les sols des pièces publiques sont décorés de façon particulièrement luxueuse.

El piso de las aéreas publicas están especialmente diseñados de manera extravagante .

La superficie del pavimento degli ambienti comuni è particolarmente elaborata.

The Peninsula

Hong Kong

The Peninsula has opened its gates to the golden twenties. The furnishing conjures up times past, such as the indoor pool, disseminating an atmosphere of Roman themes. Simultaneously, the swimmers can also throw a glance at the modern life of the city. The hotel does not only supposedly have the most generous rooms in the city but also offers the most unusual service: If desired, the guest can even be transported from the airport directly to the building roof via helicopter.

Das Peninsula hat seine Pforten in den Goldenen Zwanzigern eröffnet. Die Ausstattung beschwört vergangene Zeiten herauf, etwa im Hallenbad, das die Atmosphäre einer römischen Therme verbreitet. Gleichzeitig können die Schwimmer vom Becken aus aber auch einen Blick auf das moderne Leben der Metropole werfen. Das Hotel soll nicht nur über die geräumigsten Zimmer der Stadt verfügen, sondern auch ausgefallenen Service bieten: Auf Wunsch transportiert sogar ein Helikopter den Gast vom Flughafen direkt auf das Dach des Hauses.

Le Peninsula a ouvert ses portes dans les années 20 dorées. L'aménagement évoque les époques passées, comme par exemple dans la piscine qui rend l'ambiance de thermes romains. En même temps, les nageurs peuvent, du bassin, jeter un oeil sur la vie moderne de la métropole. L'hôtel dispose non seulement des chambres les plus spacieuses de la ville, mais offre également des services originaux : sur demande, un hélicoptère transporte même les hôtes de l'aéroport directement sur le toit de la maison.

El Peninsula abrió sus puertas en los dorados años veinte. La decoración evoca tiempos pasados, como por ejemplo la piscina cubierta que emana una atmósfera de terma romana. A la vez, desde la piscina los bañistan pueden echar un vistazo a la vida moderna de la metrópoli. El hotel no sólo dispone de las habitaciones más grandes de la ciudad, según se dice, sino que, además, ofrece servicios extraordinarios: A petición, el huésped puede incluso ser trasladado en helicóptero desde el aeropuerto directamente a la azotea del hotel.

Il Peninsula ha aperto le porte nei magnifici anni Venti. L'arredamento evoca tempi passati, per esempio la piscina coperta crea l'atmosfera di uno stabilimento termale romano. Nel contempo, però, chi nuota nella vasca può anche gettare uno sguardo sulla moderna vita della metropoli. L'hotel non solo dispone delle camere più spaziose della città, ma offre anche un servizio insolito: su richiesta addirittura un elicottero può trasferire il cliente dall'aereoporto direttamente sul tetto dell'hotel.

As the oldest and most historic luxury hotel in the former British crown colony, the Peninsula disposes over furnishings that testify to its period of origin.

Als ältestes und traditionsreichstes Luxushotel der ehemaligen britischen Kronkolonie verfügt das Peninsula über eine Ausstattung, die vom Prunk seiner Entstehungszeit zeugt.

Etant l'hôtel de luxe le plus ancien et le plus riche en traditions de l'ancienne colonie britannique, le Peninsula dispose d'un équipement qui témoigne du faste de son époque de création.

Siendo el hotel de lujo más antiguo y tradicional de la ex colonia británica, el Peninsula posee un decorado que da testimonio de la suntuosidad de la época de su creación.

Poiché si tratta dell'hotel di lusso più antico e del più ricco di tradizioni nell'ex colonia della corona britannica, il Peninsula è fornito di un arredamento che testimonia della sontuosità dell'epoca in cui sorse.

A hotel of superlatives: roomy suites with spectacular views, nine restaurants and bars, extensive wellness services and a fleet of 14 Rolls Royces are part of the equipment.

Ein Hotel der Superlative: Geräumige Suiten mit spektakulären Ausblicken, neun Restaurants und Bars, ein ausgedehntes Wellnessangebot und einem Fuhrpark von 14 Rolls Royce zählen zum Equipment.

Un hôtel au superlatif : des suites spacieuses avec des vues spectaculaires, neuf restaurants et bars, une offre wellness élargie et un parc automobile de 14 Rolls Royce font partie de l'équipement.

Un hotel de superlativos: Amplias suites con vistas espectaculares, nueve restaurantes y bares, una extensa oferta de wellness y un parque de vehículos con 14 Rolls Royce, forman parte de su equipamiento.

Un hotel dei superlativi: ampie suite con viste spettacolari, nove ristoranti e bar, un'estesa proposta wellness e un autoparco di 14 Rolls Royce fanno parte della dotazione.

A genuine surprise awaits in the highest floor. The Felix, designed by Philippe Starck, exhibits what might be his best restaurant design. At any rate, it offers the most fascinating view a restaurant can have.

Im obersten Stockwerk wartet eine echte Überraschung. Das von Philippe Starck entworfene Felix zeigt sein vielleicht bestes Restaurantdesign. Auf jeden Fall bietet es den faszinierendsten Ausblick, den ein Restaurant überhaupt haben kann.

Une vraie surprise attend à l'étage le plus élevé. Le Felix conçu par Philippe Starck montre peut-être son meilleur design de restaurant. En tout cas, il offre la vue la plus fascinante qu'un restaurant puisse avoir.

En el último piso hay una verdadera sorpresa: Tal vez el mejor diseño de restaurante del diseñador Philippe Starck: El Felix. Ofrece, en todo caso, la vista más fascinante que restaurante alguno pueda tener.

All'ultimo piano non manca una vera sorpresa. Il Felix progettato da Philippe Starck ha forse il suo miglior design per ristorante. In ogni caso offre la più affascinate vista che un ristorante possa assolutamente avere.

Grand Hyatt Plateau
Hong Kong

Despite the central location of the hotel, there is room for a 50-meter swimming pool. With its seven restaurants and bars and the 556 guestrooms, the Grand Hyatt is almost a small city in the city. The therein-integrated Plateau, a 24,000 m² wellness total work-of-art with a spa opened in the spring of 2004, as well as its own, minimalist designed rooms seem to be a village oasis.

Trotz der zentralen Lage des Hotels im dicht besiedelten Zentrum blieb noch genug Platz für ein Schwimmbad von 50 Metern Länge. Mit seinen sieben Restaurants und Bars sowie den 556 Gästezimmern ist das Grand Hyatt fast eine kleine Stadt in der Stadt. Wie eine dörfliche Oase wirkt das darin integrierte, im Frühjahr 2004 eröffnete Plateau, ein 24.000 m² großes Wellness-Gesamtkunstwerk mit Spa sowie eigenen, minimalistisch gestalteten Zimmern.

Malgré l'emplacement central de l'hôtel dans le centre très peuplé, il restait encore assez de place pour une piscine de 50 mètres de long. Avec ses huit restaurants et bars ainsi que 556 chambres, le Grand Hyatt est presque une petite ville dans la ville. Le Plateau intégré et ouvert au printemps 2004, une œuvre d'art totale wellness de 24.000 m² avec spa ainsi que ses propres chambres réalisées de façon minimaliste donnent un effet d'oasis villageois.

A pesar de su ubicación en el centro densamente poblado todavía queda suficiente espacio para una piscina de 50 metros de largo. El Grand Hyatt, con sus siete restaurantes y bares y sus 556 habitaciones, es casi como una ciudadela dentro de la ciudad. Allí está integrada el Plateau, inaugurada en la primavera de 2004, que surte el efecto de un 24,000 m² oasis rural, una obra maestra del wellness con Spa y habitaciones propias decoradas en estilo minimalista.

Nonostante la posizione centrale dell'hotel, nel centro densamente popolato, è rimasto ancora abbastanza spazio per una piscina di 50 metri di lunghezza. Con i suoi sette bar e ristoranti, nonché le 556 camere, il Grand Hyatt è quasi una piccola città nella città. Dà l'impressione di un paese o forse di un'oasi il Plateau, aperto nella primavera del 2004 e integrato nell'hotel: un centro complessivo del wellness di 24.000 m² con trattamenti termali e con camere proprie allestite in modo minimalistico.

Unflourished design significantly contributes to recuperation here. Hard to believe that one is in the middle of Hong Kong.

Schnörkelloses Design trägt hier maßgeblich zur Erholung bei. Kaum zu glauben, dass man sich mitten in Hongkong befindet.

Un design sans fioritures contribue ici dans une large mesure au repos. A peine croyable que l'on se trouve ici au centre de Hongkong.

Un diseño sobrio contribuye de manera decisiva al descanso. Apenas se puede creer que se está en medio de Hong Kong.

Un design senza fronzoli contribuisce qui in modo determinante al riposo. È difficile credere che ci si trovi in piena Hong Kong.

The panoramic harbourview from the sauna is reserved for the ladies. Guests of both genders can enjoy pleasant accommodation in the 23 rooms and suites.

Der Ausblick von der Sauna auf den Hafen ist den Damen vorbehalten. Beide Geschlechter dürfen dagegen die 23 minimalistischen Zimmer und Suiten bewohnen.

La vue du Sauna sur le port est réservée aux dames. Cependant les deux sexes peuvent habiter dans les 23 chambres et suites minimalistes.

La vista panoramica hacia el puerto desde el sauna está reservada a las damas. Por el contrario, las 23 habitaciones y suites de estilo minimalista están disponibles para ambos sexos.

La vista dalla sauna al porto è riservata alle donne. A entrambi i sessi invece è permesso abitare le 23 camere e suite minimalistiche.

Brilliant: *the architect John Edward Morford formed 25,000 m² into an aesthetic, urban recreation center.*

Gelungen: *25.000 m² hat der Architekt John Edward Morford zu einem ästhetischen, urbanen Erholungszentrum geformt.*

Réussi : *l'architecte John Edward Morford a fait des 25 000 m² un centre de repos esthétique et urbain.*

Éxito: *El arquitecto John Edward Morford ha convertido 25.000 m² en un hermoso centro de descanso urbano.*

Riuscito: *l'architetto John Edward Morford ha trasformato 25 000 m² in un centro di relax estetico e cittadino.*

Mandarin Oriental

Hong Kong

The Mandarin Oriental Hong Kong is as if made for business travelers—it lies in the middle of the banking quarter. But friends of architecture will probably also feel comfortable here as some of the best world's known high-rises, such as by Norman Foster, reach into the sky in the immediate vicinity. Most of the 541 rooms and suites offer an exciting panorama, either of the city or the nearby-situated harbor.

Wie geschaffen für Geschäftsreisende ist das Mandarin Oriental Hongkong, denn es liegt mitten im Bankenviertel. Aber auch Architekturfreunde dürften sich hier wohl fühlen, denn einige der bekanntesten Hochhäuser der Welt, etwa von Norman Foster, strecken sich in unmittelbarer Nachbarschaft dem Himmel entgegen. Die meisten der 541 Zimmer und Suiten bieten eine spannende Aussicht, entweder über die Stadt oder den nahe gelegenen Hafen.

Le Mandarin Oriental Hongkong parait avoir été créé pour les hommes d'affaires car il se situe au centre du quartier des banques. Mais les amis de l'architecture peuvent également s'y sentir bien car certains des gratte-ciels les plus connus au monde, comme par exemple de Norman Foster, s'élèvent en voisinage direct face au ciel. La plupart des 541 chambres et suites offrent une vue captivante, soit sur la ville ou sur le port situé tout près.

Como hecho a la medida para hombres y mujeres en viaje de negocios es el Mandarin Oriental Hongkong, ya que se encuentra ubicado en el centro financiero. Pero también los amantes de la arquitectura se sentirán bien aquí, puesto que algunos de los rascacielos más famosos del mundo, por ejemplo de Norman Foster, se yerguen en la inmediata vecindad. La mayoría de las 541 habitaciones y suites ofrecen una vista magnífica, de la ciudad o del cercano puerto.

Sembra fatto apposta per chi è in viaggio d'affari il Mandarin Oriental Hong Kong, perché è situato nel centro del quartiere finanziario. Ma anche gli appassionati di architettura qui potrebbero sentirsi a loro agio, infatti alcuni dei più noti grattacieli del mondo, come quello di Norman Foster, svettano contro il cielo, uno accanto all'altro. La maggior parte delle 541 camere e suite offrono una vista rilassante sulla città oppure sul vicino porto.

Modern age and antiquity: the pool, designed according to Roman models, lets one forget the skyscraper-dominated surroundings.

Neuzeit und Antike: Im Pool, der nach römischem Vorbild gestaltet ist, lässt sich die von Wolkenkratzern bestimmte Umgebung vergessen.

Nouvelle époque et antiquité : dans la piscine, réalisée selon un modèle romain, on oublie l'environnement déterminé par les gratte-ciels.

La Edad Moderna y la Antigüedad: En la piscina, diseñada a semejanza de las piscinas romanas, se olvida el entorno caracterizado por los rascacielos.

Età moderna e classica: nella piscina, allestita secondo il modello romano, si può dimenticare l'ambiente esterno caratterizzato da gratta-cieli.

Dark wooden paneling and strict furnishings breed tastefulness in the suites.

Dunkle Holzvertäfelungen und eine strenge Möblierung schaffen Gediegenheit in den Suiten.

Les sombres boiseries et un ameublement strict créent de la pureté dans les suites.

Revestimientos de madera oscura y un mobiliario austero crean una discreta elegancia en las suites.

Scuri rivestimenti in legno e mobilia severa danno alle suite un senso di solidità.

The opulent furnishings of the bars and restaurants create a magnificent ambience.

Die opulente Ausstattung der Bars und Restaurants sorgt für ein prunkvolles Ambiente.

L'aménagement opulent des bars et des restaurants garantit une ambiance fastueuse.

La opulenta decoración de los bares y restaurantes proporciona un ambiente suntuoso.

L'arredamento opulento dei bar e dei ristoranti provvede alla sontuosità dell'ambiente.

Le Meridien Cyberport

Hong Kong

The building opened in 2004 belonging to the hotel group presenting itself in refreshing high-tech luxury. Quite apparently, it would like to appeal to a younger target group that visits the Cyberport high-tech and media area. All 173 rooms are equipped with state-of-the-art electronics, including plasma screens in mural format. It can also be used as a computer monitor to quickly call up the newest data from the company computer, for example.

Das 2004 eröffnete Haus der Hotelgruppe präsentiert sich in erfrischendem High-Tech-Luxus. Ganz offensichtlich möchte es damit eine jüngere Zielgruppe ansprechen, die in dem High-Tech- und Medienviertel Cyberport verkehrt. Alle 173 Zimmer sind mit State-of-the-Art Elektronik ausgestattet, inklusive des Plasmabildschirms im Wandgemäldeformat. Er ist auch als Computermonitor nutzbar, um vom Zimmer aus zum Beispiel noch schnell die neuesten Daten vom Firmenrechner abzurufen.

Le bâtiment du groupe hôtelier ouvert en 2004 se présente dans un luxe high-tech rafraîchissant. Il souhaite ainsi attirer bien évidemment un groupe cible plus jeune qui fréquente le quartier high-tech et média Cyberport. Les 173 chambres sont équipées d'électronique de pointe, y compris l'écran plasma en format de peinture murale. Il peut également être utilisé comme écran d'ordinateur, par exemple pour consulter rapidement à partir de votre chambre les données les plus récentes de l'ordinateur de l'entreprise.

Este hotel del grupo hotelero que habrío en el 2004 se presenta con un reconfortante lujo de alta tecnología. Evidentemente se quería alcanzar un grupo meta joven, que se mueve en Cyberport, el barrio de la alta tecnología y los medios de comunicación. Todas las 173 habitaciones están dotadas con electrónica de vanguardia, inclusive pantallas plasma en formato mural. La pantalla también se puede utilizar como monitor, por ejemplo, llamar desde la habitación rápidamente los datos del ordenador de la oficina.

La filiale aperta nel 2004 si presenta in versione brioso lusso high tech. È molto evidente che ci si vorrebbe rivolgere a un target più giovane, quello che frequenta il Cyberport, il quartiere high tech e mediatico. Tutte le 173 camere sono fornite di un impianto elettronico di ultima generazione, comprensivo dello schermo al plasma alla parete; il quale è utilizzabile anche come monitor per il computer, per esempio, per richiamare ancora alla svelta gli ultimi dati del calcolatore della ditta persino in camera d'albergo.

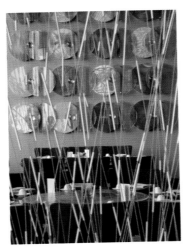 

Richly colored decoration defines the interior architecture as here in one of the corridors or in the Nam Fong restaurant, waiting with Cantonese cuisine. From the pool, one overlooks the bay.

Farbenprächtige Dekore bestimmen die Innenarchitektur, wie hier in einem der Flure oder im Restaurant Nam Fong, das mit kantonesischer Küche aufwartet. Vom Pool aus überblickt man die Bucht.

Les décors aux couleurs foncées déterminent l'architecture intérieure, comme ici dans l'un des couloirs ou dans le restaurant Nam Fong qui sert de la cuisine cantonaise. De la piscine, on embrasse la baie du regard.

Una decoración en colores fuertes determina la arquitectura interior, como aquí en uno de los pasillos o en el restaurante Nam Fong, que ofrece cocina cantonesa. Desde la piscina se puede observar la bahía.

Decorazioni dai colori forti caratterizzano l'architettura interna, come in uno dei corridoi o nel ristorante Nam Fong, che offre cucina cantonese. Dalla piscina si abbraccia con lo sguardo la baia.

Lobby, lounge and bar in the ground floor with their backdrop-like design immediately signalize the operator's desire to set its building into the scene as a lifestyle temple.

Lobby, Lounge und Bar im Erdgeschoss signalisieren mit ihrer kulissenartigen Gestaltung sofort den Anspruch der Betreiber, ihr Haus als Lifestyletempel in Szene zu setzen.

Le hall, le salon et le bar au rez-de-chaussée signalent avec leur aménagement semblable à des coulisses l'exigence du propriétaire de mettre son hôtel en scène tel un temple de style de vie.

El vestíbulo, el lounge y el bar en la planta baja ya dan a entender con su diseño escenográfico el propósito de la gerencia: Presentarse como templo del lifestyle.

Ingresso, lounge e bar al piano terra con il loro allestimento scenografico segnalano subito la pretesa del gestore di far apparire il suo hotel come un tempio del nuovo stile di vita.

The guest has a view to the ocean not only from the bed and but also from the bathtub.

Sowohl vom Bett als auch von der freistehenden Wanne im verglasten Baderaum aus kann der Gast über den Ozean schauen.

L'hôte peut regarder l'océan de son lit comme de la baignoire indépendante dans la salle de bains au toit en verre.

Tanto desde la cama como desde la bañera no empotrada en el baño revestido de cristal, el huésped tiene vista hacia el océano.

Sia dal letto sia dalla vasca non murata – in un bagno dalle pareti vetrate – l'ospite può posare lo sguardo sull'oceano.

Le Meridien Cyberport *Hong Kong* 159

Les Suites Taipei

Taipei, Taiwan

In both buildings, conducted as a unit, maintaining an exemplary, private atmosphere in the public areas has been accomplished. There are recreational, work, and conference rooms in which the interior architecture reminds one more of a modern villa than a hotel, achieved through organized layouts, furniture, and material and color selection. The libraries, furnished with a remarkable number of art and photography books contribute greatly to this.

In den beiden als Einheit geführten Häusern ist es beispielhaft gelungen, private Atmosphäre in den öffentlichen Räumen zu bewahren. So gibt es Aufenthalts-, Arbeits- und Konferenzräume, deren Innenarchitektur durch geschickte Grundrisse, Möblierung, Material- und Farbauswahl eher an eine moderne Villa als an ein Hotel erinnern. Großen Anteil daran haben die mit beachtlich vielen Kunst- und Fotobänden ausgestatteten Bibliotheken.

Dans les deux bâtiments fonctionnant comme une unité, la réussite a été de conserver une atmosphère privée dans les pièces publiques. Il y a ainsi des salles de séjour, de travail et de conférence dont l'architecture intérieure rappelle plutôt une villa moderne qu'un hôtel par ses plans habiles, son ameublement, le choix des matériaux et des couleurs. Les bibliothèques comprenant de nombreux et remarquables ouvrages d'art et de photographie jouent également un grand rôle.

En las dos edificaciones que constituyen una unidad se ha logrado de manera ejemplar conservar una atmósfera privada en los espacios públicos. Así, entonces, hay salones de estancia, salas de trabajo y de conferencias cuyo diseño interior asemeja chalés modernos, más que un hotel tradicional. Esto es logrado con la elección del mobiliario, materiales y colores. Los espacios bibliotecarios de considerable cantidad de tomos de arte y fotografía contribuyen al igual con el concepto.

Nei due edifici, da intendere come un'unità, si è riusciti magistralmente a mantenere negli spazi comuni un'atmosfera da abitazione privata. Così ci sono sale di ritrovo, studi, sale per conferenze, la cui architettura d'interni ricorda più una villa moderna che un hotel, grazie alle accorte planimetrie, all'arredamendo e alla scelta di materiali e di colori. Grande parte in questo hanno le biblioteche notevolmente fornite di molti volumi d'arte e di fotografìa.

Reduced forms and warm colors and materials create a living room atmosphere in both buildings. The owner's passion for photography finds expression in the wall decoration.

Reduzierte Formen sowie warme Farben und Materialien erzeugen in beiden Häusern Wohnzimmeratmosphäre. Die Leidenschaft des Eigentümers für Fotografie schlägt sich auch in den Wanddekorationen nieder.

Des formes réduites ainsi que des couleurs et des matériaux chauds créent dans les deux bâtiments une atmosphère de salle de séjour. La passion du propriétaire pour la photographie se retrouve également dans les décorations murales.

Formas sobrias, así como colores y materiales cálidos, generan en ambas edificaciones un ambiente acogedor. La pasión del propietario por la fotografía se refleja en la decoración de las paredes.

Sobrietà delle forme ma anche colori e materiali caldi producono in entrambi gli edifici atmosfere da salotto privato. La passione del proprietario per la fotografia si riflette anche nelle decorazioni delle pareti.

In larger of the two buildings on the Da-an Road, 90 rooms are organized around a seven-storey high atrium, with the "Living Room" library and bar being the main attraction.

Im größeren Haus in der Da-an Road sind die 90 Zimmer um ein siebengeschossiges Atrium verteilt. Mittelpunkt ist der „Living Room" mit Bibliothek und Bar.

Dans la maison la plus grande de la Da-an Road, les 90 chambres sont réparties autour d'un atrium de sept étages. Le point central est le « Living Room » avec la bibliothèque et le bar.

En la casa más grande, en el Da-an Road, las 90 habitaciones se distribuyen alrededor de un atrio que abarca siete pisos. Punto central es el "Living Room", con biblioteca y bar.

Nell'edificio più grande, nella Da-an Road, le 90 camere sono distribuite intorno ad un atrio di sette piani. Punto centrale è il "Living Room" con biblioteca e bar.

Baths in marble without any curlicues. Simplicity also reigns in the room furnishings. Almost all the furniture was specially designed for the hotel.

Baden in Marmor einmal ganz ohne Schnörkel. Schlichtheit herrscht auch bei der Ausstattung der Zimmer. Fast alle Möbel sind speziell für das Hotel entworfen.

Prendre une fois son bain dans du marbre, sans fioritures. La simplicité domine également dans l'aménagement de la chambre. Presque tous les meubles ont été conçus spécialement pour l'hôtel.

Baños de mármol completamente sobrios. La sencillez predomina también en la decoración de las habitaciones. Casi todo el mobiliario fue diseñado especialmente para el hotel.

Farsi un bagno nel marmo senza fronzoli assolutamente. La semplicità domina anche nell'arredamento delle camere. Quasi tutti i mobili sono stati ideati appositamente per l'hotel.

The Lalu

Sun Moon Lake, Taiwan

Asian inspired minimalism defines the aesthetic concept of the hotel on the banks on the glassy Sun Moon Lake. Stressed travelers find relaxation here. Sliding doors covered with rice paper open up to the tropical private gardens of suites and villas. Crackling fireplaces and a gentle color scheme from jade green to mahogany brown support the meditative style, created by the architect Kerry Hill. Nature shows its mysterious side here. The lake, it is told, has magical powers.

Asiatisch inspirierter Minimalismus bestimmt das ästhetische Konzept des Hotels am Ufer des spiegelglatten Sun Moon Lake. Gestresste Reisende finden hier Entspannung. Mit Reispapier bespannte Schiebetüren öffnen sich zu den tropischen Privatgärten der Suiten und Villen. Prasselnde Kaminfeuer und eine sanfte Farbpalette von Jadegrün bis Mahagonibraun unterstützen den meditativen Stil, den Architekt Kerry Hill kreierte. Die Natur zeigt hier ihre geheimnisvolle Seite. Der See, so wird erzählt, hat magische Kräfte.

Le minimalisme inspiré de l'art asiatique détermine le concept esthétique de l'hôtel sur la rive du Sun Moon Lake, lisse comme un miroir. Les voyageurs stressés trouveront ici une atmosphère de détente. Avec des portes coulissantes recouvertes de papier de riz, les suites et les villas s'ouvrent aux jardins privés tropicaux. Le feu de cheminée crépitant et une douce palette de couleurs de vert jade à brun acajou encouragent le style méditatif que l'architecte Kerry Hill créa. La nature montre ici son coté mystérieux. Le lac a, raconte-t-on, des forces magiques.

Un minimalismo asiático determina el concepto estético del hotel a orillas del Sun Moon Lake, tan liso como un espejo. Los viajeros estresados encuentran aquí relajamiento. Puertas corredizas revestidas de papel de arroz se abren hacia los jardines tropicales privados de las suites y los chalés. Fuego crujiente en la chimenea y una gama de colores que va del verde jade hasta el marrón caoba contribuyen al estilo meditativo que creó el arquitecto Kerry Hill. La naturaleza muestra aquí su lado más misterioso. El lago, se dice, tiene poderes mágicos.

Minimalismo di ispirazione asiatica caratterizza la concezione estetica dell'hotel sulle sponde del Sun Moon Lake liscio come uno specchio. I viaggiatori stressati qui trovano il loro relax. Porte scorrevoli rivestite con carta di riso si aprono sui giardini tropicali interni delle suite e delle ville. Camini dai fuochi scoppiettanti e una tavolozza di colori tenui dal verde giada al mogano sottolineano lo stile meditativo creato dall'architetto Kerry Hill. La natura mostra qui il suo lato misterioso. Il lago, così si racconta, ha magiche energie.

Wood, stone, and glass are the dominant materials. Slat constructions relax the surfaces and create transparency.

Holz, Stein und Glas sind die dominierenden Materialien. Lattenkonstruktionen lockern die Flächen auf und schaffen Transparenz.

Bois, pierre et verre sont les matériaux dominants. Les constructions en lattis adoucissent les surfaces et créent de la transparence.

Madera, piedra y cristal son los materiales predominantes. Construcciones de tablas aligeran las superficies y crean transparencia.

Legno, pietra e vetro sono i materiali dominanti. Le costruzioni a listelli hanno superfici mosse e creano trasparenze.

Pure architecture. What might appear too cool for some excites others: a bath in this puristic stone bath-tub or a massage with a view of Sun Moon Lake.

Architektur pur. Was manchen vielleicht etwas zu kühl erscheinen mag, versetzt andere in Hochstimmung: ein Bad in dieser puristischen Steinwanne oder eine Massage mit Blick auf den Sun Moon Lake.

De l'architecture pure. Ce que certains trouveront peut-être un peu trop froid, en enthousiasmera d'autres : un bain dans cette baignoire puriste en pierre ou un massage avec vue sur le Sun Moon Lake.

Arquitectura pura: Lo que a algunos tal vez les parezca algo frío, a otros les entusiasma: Tomar un baño en esta bañera purista de piedra o un masaje con vista al Sun Moon Lake.

Pura architettura. Ciò che ad alcuni può apparire un po' troppo freddo, mette di ottimo umore altri: un bagno in questa puristica vasca in pietra oppure un massaggio con vista sul Sun Moon Lake.

The guests can choose from among five restaurants and bars. The Japanese restaurant and the Oriental Brasserie among them.

Fünf Restaurants und Bars stehen den Gästen zur Wahl. Darunter The Japanese Restaurant oder The Oriental Brasserie.

Cinq restaurants et bars sont au choix des hôtes. Parmi eux, The Japanese restaurant ou The Oriental Brasserie.

Cinco restaurantes y bares para que los huéspedes elijan. Entre ellos, el restaurante The Japanese o la The Oriental Brasserie .

Gli ospiti hanno la scelta tra cinque bar e ristoranti. Tra questi il ristorante The Japanese o la The Oriental Brasserie.

Whether in the president's villa, the pool villas, or in the suites, the guests find markedly much space, air, light, and always have a view of the lake.

Ob in der Präsidentenvilla, den Poolvillen oder in den Suiten, die Gäste finden ausgesprochen viel Platz, Luft, Licht und haben stets Aussicht auf den See.

Que ce soit dans la villa présidentielle, les villas de la piscine ou les suites, les hôtes trouvent extrêmement beaucoup de place, d'air, de lumière et ont toujours vue sur le lac.

Sea en el chalé presidencial, en los chalés de la piscina o en las suites, los huéspedes tienen mucho espacio, aire y luz y siempre tienen vista del lago.

Nella villa presidenziale, come nelle ville con piscina o nelle suite gli ospiti trovano decisamente molta luce, aria e spazio e hanno sempre la vista sul lago.

Mojiko Hotel

Mochi, Japan

The Mojiko lies directly at the water, so that the guests can view the happenings in the harbor from their rooms. It is one of the last works by the Italian architect Aldo Rossi and entailed a planning duration of eleven years. Together with Shigero Uchida, responsible for the interior decoration, Rossi designed the hotel as a mixture of European and Japanese architecture. The restaurants, bars and rooms for the Japanese tea ceremony are open to the neighborhood.

Das Mojiko liegt direkt am Wasser, sodass die Gäste von ihren Zimmern aus das Geschehen am Hafen beobachten können. Es ist eines der letzten Werke des italienischen Architekten Aldo Rossi und nahm eine Planungsdauer von elf Jahren in Anspruch. Zusammen mit Shigero Uchida, der für die Innenarchitektur verantwortlich zeichnete, entwarf Rossi das Hotel als eine Mischung aus europäischer und japanischer Architektur. Die Restaurants, Bars und Räume für die japanische Teezeremonie stehen auch der Nachbarschaft offen.

Le Mojiko se trouve juste au bord de l'eau de telle sorte à ce que les hôtes puissent observer de leurs chambres ce qui se passe au port. Il s'agit de l'une des dernières œuvres de l'architecte italien Aldo Rossi qui nécessita une durée de planification de onze ans. Avec Shigero Uchida, qui etait responsable de l'architecture intérieure, Rossi a conçu l'hôtel comme un mélange d'architecture européenne et japonaise. Les restaurants, bars et pièces pour la cérémonie du thé japonaise sont également ouverts au voisinage.

El Mojiko se encuentra al lado del mar, de tal forma que los huéspedes pueden observar desde sus habitaciones el movimiento del puerto. Es una de las últimas obras del arquitecto italiano Aldo Rossi, y su planificación tardó once años. Junto a Shigero Uchida, responsable de la arquitectura interior, Rossi diseñó el hotel como una combinación de arquitectura europea y japonesa. Los restaurantes, bares y salones para la ceremonia del té japonesa están abiertos al público.

Il Mojiko è situata direttamente sull'acqua, cosicché gli ospiti dalle loro camere possono osservare la vita nel porto. È una delle ultime opere dell'architetto italiano Aldo Rossi e ha richiesto una progettazione di undici anni. Insieme a Shigero Uchida, responsabile degli architettura interni, Aldo Rossi ha concepito l'hotel come un misto di architettura europea e giapponese. I ristoranti, i bar e i locali per la cerimonia giapponese del tè sono aperti anche agli esterni.

While the bistro is rather austerely designed, the room for the tea ceremony evokes the traditional Japanese architectural motifs.

Während das Bistro eher nüchtern gestaltet ist, lässt der Raum für die Teezeremonie Motive traditioneller japanischer Architektur anklingen.

Alors que le café est réalisé de façon plutôt simple, la pièce pour la cérémonie du thé fait appel à des motifs de l'architecture traditionnelle japonaise.

Mientras que el bistró tiene una decoración bastante neutral, el salón para la ceremonia del té presenta elementos de la arquitectura japonesa tradicional.

Mentre il bistrot ha piuttosto un aspetto essenziale, il locale per la cerimonia del tè riecheggia motivi dell'architettura giapponese tradizionale.

The suites under the roof are furnished in European style; but some guestrooms exude classical Japanese asceticism.

Die Suiten unter dem Dach sind im europäischen Stil eingerichtet, einige Gästezimmer verströmen hingegen klassische japanische Askese.

Les suites sous le toit sont aménagées dans un style européen, quelques chambres répandent en revanche l'ascèse classique japonaise.

Las suites del último piso están decoradas en estilo europeo, algunas habitaciones, por el contrario, emanan el clásico ascetismo japonés.

Le suite del sottotetto sono arredate in stile europeo, alcune camere invece diffondono un clima da ascesi giapponese classica.

Niki Club

Nasu Gun, Japan

Uncompromising modern architecture, interspersed with light Japanese influences characterizes the resort. Massive exposed concrete walls meet up with filigree sliding partitions, wooden floors with tatami mats. Adapted from traditional Japanese Ryokan are small private gardens that slide like a glass partition as a tiny atrium between the living and sleeping areas of the suites. The 19 accommodations are placed across several mini-villas, so that the facility resembles a small village.

Eine kompromisslos moderne Architektur, durchsetzt mit leichten japanischen Einflüssen, prägt das Resort. Wuchtige Sichtbetonmauern treffen auf filigrane Schiebewände, Holzböden auf Tatamimatten. Den traditionellen japanischen Ryokan nachempfunden sind die kleinen Privatgärten, die sich wie ein verglaster Raumteiler als winziges Atrium zwischen Wohn- und Schlafbereich der Suiten schieben. Die 19 Unterkünfte des Resorts verteilen sich auf mehrere Minivillen, so dass die Anlage an ein kleines Dorf erinnert.

Une architecture moderne sans compromis, intégrant de légères influences japonaises, caractérise l'hôtel de tourisme. Des murs massifs en béton brut rencontrent des murs coulissants filigranes, des sols en bois sur des tatamis. Les petits jardins privés sont inspirés des traditionnels Ryokan japonais que l'on pousse comme une séparation en verre pour former un minuscule atrium entre le séjour et la chambre à coucher des suites. Les 19 logements de l'hôtel de tourisme se répartissent sur plusieurs petites villas, si bien que le site rappelle un petit village.

Una arquitectura moderna que no hace concesiones, en combinación con ligeros acentos japoneses, caracteriza el resort. Macizos muros expuestos de hormigón se unen a paredes corredizas afiligranadas, suelos de madera a esteras tatami. A semejanza del Ryokan tradicional japonés son diseñados los pequeños jardines privados, que como un diminuto atrio se deslizan como una división de cristal entre las salas de estar y las habitaciones de las suites. Las 19 habitaciones del resort se distribuyen en varios mini chalés, de tal forma que el complejo evoca un pequeño pueblo.

Un'architettura moderna senza compromessi, contaminata appena da influssi giapponesi, caratterizza il resort. Massicci muri in calcestruzzo a vista fanno contrasto con pareti scorrevoli in filigrana, pavimenti di legno con tatami. Ispirati ai tradizionali ryokan giapponesi sono i piccoli giardini privati, che si insinuano tra zona giorno e zona notte delle suite come elemento divisorio chiuso da una vetrata, una sorta di minuscolo atrio. Le 19 sistemazioni del resort sono distribuite su più miniville, cosicché la struttura ricorda un piccolo villaggio.

Located only one hour from hectic Tokyo, the Niki Club offers quiet between wooded hills.

Nur eine gute Stunde vom hektischen Tokio entfernt, bietet der Niki Club Ruhe zwischen bewaldeten Hügeln.

Situé seulement à une bonne heure de la ville trépidante de Tokyo, le Niki Club offre du calme ente les collines boisées.

Apenas a una hora de distancia del trajin de Tokio, el Niki Club ofrece tranquilidad entre las boscosas colinas.

A poco più di un'ora dalla frenetica Tokyo, il Niki Club offre tranquillità e pace tra colline boscose.

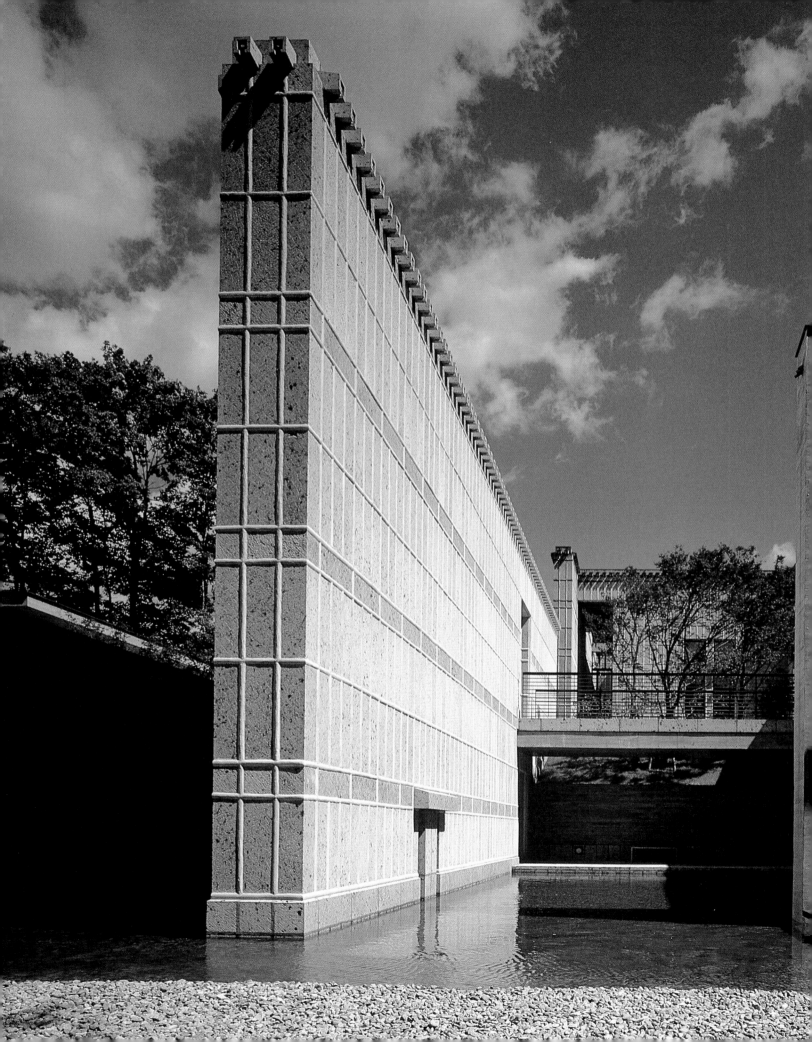

Room-high, *partially frameless glazing, create a flowing transition from indoors to outdoors.*

Raumhohe, *zum Teil rahmenlose Verglasungen schaffen einen fließenden Übergang von innen nach außen.*

Des verreries *hautes comme la pièce, parfois sans encadrement, créent une transition floue de l'intérieur à l'extérieur.*

Ventanales *de gran altura, en parte sin marco, crean una transición fluida de adentro hacia afuera.*

Vetrate a *tutt'altezza, in parte senza intelaiatura, rendono fluido il passaggio tra dentro e fuori.*

Park Hyatt Tokyo
Tokyo, Japan

"Lost in translation", this film made the hotel world-famous in 2003. The bar, pool, and suites served as backdrops for the most important scenes in the subtle love story. The Park Hyatt lies in the fourteen upper floors of a skyscraper designed by Kenzo Tange. Along with the spectacular views of the largest city in the world, the 178 hotel rooms offer pure luxury and a lot of space in the metropolis bursting from its seams. They suppose to be the largest in the city.

„Lost in translation" – dieser Film machte das Hotel im Jahr 2003 weltberühmt. Für die wichtigsten Szenen der subtilen Liebesgeschichte dienten die Bar, der Pool und die Suiten als Kulisse. Das Park Hyatt liegt in den vierzehn obersten Stockwerken eines Wolkenkratzers, den Kenzo Tange entwarf. Neben den spektakulären Ausblicken auf die größte Stadt der Welt bieten die 178 Hotelzimmer etwas, das in der engen, aus allen Nähten platzenden Metropole wahrer Luxus ist: viel Platz. Sie sollen die größten der Stadt sein.

« Lost in translation » – ce film a rendu l'hôtel célèbre en 2003. Le bar, la piscine et les suites ont servi de coulisses pour les scènes les plus importantes de la subtile histoire d'amour. Le Park Hyatt se trouve dans les quatorze étages supérieurs d'un gratte-ciel conçu par Kenzo Tange. Parallèlement aux vues spectaculaires sur la ville la plus grande du monde, les 178 chambres de l'hôtel offrent quelque chose qui est un vrai luxe dans la métropole étroite et qui explose littéralement : beaucoup de place. Elles seraient les plus grandes de la ville.

"Lost in translation" está película hizo mundialmente famoso al hotel en el 2003. Para las escenas más importantes de esta sutil historia de amor se utilizaron como escenarios el bar, la piscina y suites. El Park Hyatt se encuentra en los últimos catorce pisos de un rascacielos diseñado por Kenzo Tange. Junto a las espectaculares vistas de la ciudad más grande del mundo, las 178 habitaciones ofrecen algo que es un verdadero lujo en esta metrópoli densamente poblada: Mucho espacio. Se dice que son las habationes más grandes de la ciudad.

"Lost in translation" é il film che nel 2003 ha reso l'hotel famoso nel mondo. Per le più importanti scene della complessa storia d'amore il bar, la piscina e le suite hanno fatto da scenografia. Il Park Hyatt si trova sugli ultimi quattordici piani di un grattacielo progettato da Kenzo Tange. Oltre alle spettacolari vedute sulla più grande città del mondo, le 178 camere dell'hotel offrono qualcosa che in quella metropoli angusta, ormai sul punto di scoppiare, è un vero lusso: molto spazio. Dovrebbero essere le più grandi della città.

The floor to ceiling windows in the indoor swimming pool and restaurant allow views of the bursting activities in the streets of Tokyo and of Mount Fuji, if the sky is clear.

Die raumhohe Verglasung im Hallenbad und in den Restaurants gestattet Ausblicke auf das quirlige Treiben in den Straßen Tokios und – bei gutem Wetter – auf den Fuji.

Le vitrage aussi haut que la pièce dans la piscine couverte et dans les restaurants offre une vue sur la vie turbulente dans les rues de Tokyo et – par beau temps – sur le mont Fuji.

Los altos ventanales en la piscina cubierta y en los restaurantes permiten observar el vivo trajín de las calles de Tokio y con tiempo despejado el Fujiyama.

Le vetrate a tutt'altezza permettono nella piscina coperta e nei ristoranti la vista sul vivacissimo viavai delle strade di Tokyo e se il tempo è bello sul Fuji.

Exquisite interior: *modern art is not only present in the public zones, but thrughout the hotel guest rooms and bathrooms; a mahogany staircase connects the rooms in the conference area with the lobby.*

Exquisite Interieurs: *Moderne Kunst gibt es nicht nur in den öffentlichen Zonen, sondern auch in den Bädern; eine Mahagonitreppe verbindet die Räume im Konferenzbereich mit der Lobby.*

Intérieurs raffinés : *l'art moderne ne se trouve pas seulement dans les zones publiques, mais également dans les salles de bains ; un escalier en acajou relie les pièces de conférences au hall.*

Interiores exquisitos: *Arte moderno no sólo en las áreas públicas, sino también en los baños; una escalera de caoba une los salones del área de conferencias con el vestíbulo.*

Raffinati interni: *l'arte moderna non si trova solo negli spazi comuni, ma anche nei bagni; una scala di mogano collega le sale della zona conferenze con il salone centrale.*

Four Seasons Hotel Tokyo at Marunouchi

Tokyo, Japan

The smallest hotel in the group is located next to Tokyo Station in the lower floors of an office building. Its only 57 rooms are furnished in 17 different ways so that a guest who visits the hotel a second time has a good chance of gaining totally new impressions. In those rooms that have good views, there is a bathtub made of limestone in front of the floor level windows. A dreamland for train lovers, who can watch the express trains pulling in and out from there.

Direkt neben der Tokio Station befindet sich das kleinste Haus der Gruppe in den unteren Stockwerken eines Büroturms. Seine nur 57 Zimmer sind auf 17 unterschiedliche Arten eingerichtet, sodass ein Gast, der das Hotel ein zweites Mal besucht, gute Chancen auf ganz neue Eindrücke hat. In denjenigen Zimmern, die eine gute Aussicht bieten, steht eine Badewanne aus Kalkstein vor den bodentiefen Fenstern. Ein Schlaraffenland für Eisenbahn-Liebhaber, die von dort die ein- und ausfahrenden Expresszüge beobachten können.

Juste à côté de Tokyo Station se trouve le plus petit hôtel du groupe dans les étages les plus inférieurs d'une tour de bureaux. Ses chambres, seulement 57, sont aménagées de 17 façons différentes, si bien qu'un hôte qui fréquente l'hôtel une deuxième fois a de bonnes chances de ressentir de toutes nouvelles impressions. Dans les chambres qui offrent une belle vue se trouve une baignoire en calcaire devant les fenêtres atteignant le sol. Un pays de cocagne pour les amoureux des chemins de fer qui peuvent observer de cet endroit les trains express à l'arrivée et au départ.

Justo al lado de la estación de ferrocarril de Tokio se encuentra la más pequeña de las construcciones del grupo hotelero, en los primeros pisos de una torre de oficinas. Sus 57 habitaciones están decoradas de 17 maneras diferentes, de tal forma que quien visita el hotel por segunda vez tiene buenas probabilidades de llevarse una impresión totalmente nueva. En las habitaciones que tienen una buena vista hay una bañera de piedra caliza frente a las ventanas que llegan hasta el suelo. Un paraíso para los amantes del ferrocarril que pueden observar así las llegadas y salidas de los trenes expresos.

Proprio accanto alla stazione di Tokyo si trova il più piccolo hotel del gruppo, situato ai piani inferiori di una torre per uffici. Le sole 57 camere sono arredate in diciassette modi differenti, cosicché un cliente che torna di nuovo nell'hotel ha buone possibilità di ricevere impressioni completamente nuove. In quelle camere che offrono una buona vista, una vasca da bagno in calcare è posta davanti alle finestre che arrivano fino al pavimento. Una cuccagna per gli appassionati di ferrovie: da lì si possono osservare i treni che vanno e vengono.

Quiet and a stately ambience greet the visitor who enters the hotel situated in the Marunouchi financial and business district. The shopping paradise of Ginza is also within walking distance.

Ruhe und ein gediegenes Ambiente empfangen den Besucher, der das im Finanz- und Geschäftsviertel Marunouchi gelegene Hotel betritt. Das Shoppingparadies von Ginza ist zudem in Fußweite.

Le calme et une ambiance pure reçoivent le visiteur qui entre dans l'hôtel situé dans le quartier des affaires et des finances Marunouchi. De plus, le paradis du shopping de Ginza est accessible à pied.

Tranquilidad y un ambiente puro esperan al visitante que entra al hotel ubicado en el sector financiero y de negocios, Marunouchi. El paraíso del shopping, Ginza, se encuentra a un paso de distancia.

Tranquillità e un ambiente curato accolgono l'ospite, che entra nell'hotel situato a Marunouchi, il quartiere commerciale e finanziario. Per di più Ginza, il paradiso dello shopping, è raggiungibile a piedi.

Contrast *as principle: dark against light surfaces in the rooms, vertical wood grain contra horizontal stone cladding in the lobby lounge.*

Kontrast *als Prinzip: dunkle gegen helle Oberflächen in den Zimmern, vertikale Holzmaserung kontra horizontale Steinverkleidung in der Lobby Lounge.*

Le contraste *comme principe : surfaces sombres contre surfaces claires dans les chambres, veinure en bois verticale contre revêtement en pierre horizontale dans le lobby lounge.*

Contraste *como principio: Superficies claras y oscuras en las habitaciones, veta de madera verticale y revestimiento de piedra horizontal en el lounge del vestíbulo.*

Il contrasto *come principio: nelle camere le superfici scure contro le chiare, nel lounge dell'atrio le venature del legno in verticale contro il rivestimento di pietra in orizzontale.*

Moderate modernism: *the furnishing opposes the pulsating life at the door with a design concept of soft tones.*

Moderate Modernität: *Die Einrichtung setzt dem pulsierenden Leben vor der Tür ein Gestaltungskonzept der leisen Töne entgegen.*

Modernité modérée : *l'aménagement oppose à la vie bouillonnante se trouvant devant la porte un concept de réalisation de tons légers.*

Modernidad sobria: *Una decoración de diseño suave y ligero se contrapone a la vida animada de la calle.*

Modernità moderatamente: *l'arredamento oppone alla vita pulsante dietro la porta una concezione progettuale dai toni lievi.*

The Strings Hotel

Tokyo, Japan

The hotel opened in 2003 presents itself in contemporary architecture. Its 206 rooms surround an atrium, spread across the seven highest floors of the skyscraper. The heart of the hotel is a large water basin with black pebbles on the bottom, from which a contemplative mood exudes. One of the two restaurants shifts like a peninsula over the water surface and is accessible via a glass bridge. The other offers a panoramic view over the Bay of Tokyo.

In zeitgenössischer Architektur präsentiert sich das 2003 eröffnete Hotel. Seine 206 Zimmer umschließen ein Atrium, das sich über die sieben obersten Stockwerke eines Hochhauses verteilt. Herz des Hotels ist ein großes Wasserbecken mit schwarzen Kieselsteinen am Boden, von dem eine kontemplative Stimmung ausgeht. Eines der beiden Restaurants schiebt sich wie eine Halbinsel über die Wasserfläche und ist über eine gläserne Brücke erreichbar. Das andere bietet einen Panoramablick über die Tokioter Bucht.

L'hôtel ouvert en 2003 se présente avec une architecture contemporaine. Ses 206 chambres entourent un atrium qui se répartit sur les sept étages supérieurs d'un gratte-ciel. Le cœur de l'hôtel est un grand bassin d'eau avec des cailloux noirs au fond et duquel se dégage une ambiance de contemplation. L'un des deux restaurants se fraie, tel une presqu'île, un chemin sur la surface de l'eau et est accessible par un pont en verre. L'autre offre une vue panoramique sur la baie de Tokyo.

El hotel inaugurado en 2003 se presenta con una arquitectura contemporánea. Sus 206 habitaciones se encuentran alrededor del atrio, que abarca los últimos siete pisos de un rascacielos. El corazón del hotel es una gran piscina con fondo de pedernal negro, de donde emana un ánimo contemplativo. Uno de los dos restaurantes se desliza como una península sobre la superficie del agua y a él se accede atravesando un puente de cristal. El otro ofrece una vista panorámica de la bahía de Tokio.

In chiave contemporanea si presenta l'architettura dell'hotel aperto nel 2003. Le 206 camere circondano un atrio, che si distribuisce sugli ultimi sette piani di un grattacielo. Cuore dell'hotel è una grande vasca d'acqua con ciottoli neri sul fondo, dalla quale emana un'atmosfera contemplativa. Uno dei due ristoranti si spinge come una penisola sulla superficie dell'acqua ed è raggiungibile da un ponte di vetro. L'altro offre una vista panoramica sulla baia di Tokyo.

Purism and aesthetic restrain define the reception, rooms, and atrium.

Purismus und gestalterische Zurückhaltung prägen Rezeption, Zimmer und Atrium.

Purisme et réserve dans la réalisation caractérisent la réception, les chambres et l'atrium.

Purismo y moderación caracterizan la recepción, las habitaciones y el atrio.

Purismo e forme discrete caratterizzano reception, camere e atrio.

One's gaze can wander across the skyline and Bay of Tokyo.

Von den Zimmern aus kann der Blick über die Skyline und die Tokioter Bucht schweifen.

Des chambres, le regard peut errer sur les gratte-ciels et la baie de Tokyo.

Desde las habitaciones se pueden observar el skyline y la bahía de Tokio.

Dalle camere lo sguardo può spaziare dallo skyline alla baia di Tokyo.

Building resistance *to a fear of heights: through the room-high glazing, guests can look deep down into the business district around the Shinagawa train station.*

Abhärtungsprogramm *gegen Höhenangst: Durch die raumhohe Verglasung können die Gäste tief nach unten in das Geschäftsviertel um den Bahnhof Shinagawa schauen.*

Le programme d'endurcissement *contre le vertige : grâce aux vitrages hauts comme les pièces, les hôtes peuvent regarder tout en bas vers le quartier des affaires situé autour de la gare Shinagawa.*

Terapia de choque *contra el vértigo: A través de los altos ventanales los huéspedes pueden observar la zona comercial de los alrededores de la estación de ferrocarril Shinagawa.*

Terapia d'urto *contro le vertigini: attraverso le vetrate a tutt'altezza gli ospiti possono guardare giù verso Shinagawa, il quartiere commerciale intorno alla stazione.*

Hotel Lindrum

Melbourne, Australia

In the midst of Melbourne directly on the Yarra River lies the hotel in an old warehouse from 1900. The building served as the headquarters of a daily newspaper and then turned into a billiard club run by the Lindrum family from which a few billiard champions descended and after whom the hotel is named. Fortunately much of the building's old charm was preserved during renovation as modern design was complemented very cautiously so that the lounges now seem to be lofts.

Mitten in Melbourne, direkt am Yarra River, liegt das Hotel in einem alten Lagergebäude aus dem Jahr 1900. Der Bau diente auch einmal als Hauptquartier einer Tageszeitung, bevor er sich in einen Billardclub verwandelte. Dieser wurde von der Familie Lindrum betrieben, der einige Billardchampions entstammen und nach der das heutige Hotel benannt ist. Beim Umbau blieb glücklicherweise viel vom alten Charme des Gebäudes erhalten, weil modernes Design sehr behutsam ergänzt wurde, sodass die Gästezimmer heute wie Lofts wirken.

L'hôtel se trouve au centre de Melbourne, au bord de la rivière Yarra, dans un ancien entrepôt de 1900. Le bâtiment servit autrefois également de quartier principal d'un journal quotidien avant de se transformer en club de billard. Celui-ci était exploité par la famille Lindrum dont sont issus quelques champions de billard et dont le nom a été donné à l'hôtel actuel. Lors des transformations, la plupart de l'ancien charme des bâtiments a été heureusement conservé car le design moderne a été complété avec grande précaution, si bien que les chambres des hôtes font aujourd'hui l'effet de lofts.

En el centro de Melbourne, a orillas del río Yarra, se ubica el hotel en un antiguo depósito de 1900. La construcción sirvió también alguna vez como oficina central de un diario, antes de convertirse en un club de billar. Éste fue dirigido por la familia Lindrum, que da nombre al hotel, y de la cual provienen algunos campeones de billar. Afortunadamente al hacer la remodelación se conservó mucho del encanto original de la construcción, gracias a que el diseño moderno se integró de manera muy discreta, de tal forma que las habitaciones parecen lofts.

Nel centro di Melbourne, direttamente sul fiume Yarra, l'hotel si trova in un vecchio magazzino che risale al 1900. L'edificio una volta serviva anche da quartier generale di un quotidiano, prima di trasformarsi in un circolo di biliardo. Quest'ultimo era gestito dalla famiglia Lindrum, dalla quale provengono alcuni campioni di biliardo e dalla quale l'odierno hotel prende il nome. Nella ristrutturazione per fortuna è stato preservato il vecchio charme dell'edificio, dato che il design moderno è stato integrato con molta cautela, e così oggi le camere sembrano dei loft.

Historical architecture and an old billiard table nudge up to restrained modern furniture.

Historische Architektur und ein alter Billardtisch stoßen auf eine maßvoll moderne Einrichtung.

Une architecture historique et une ancienne table de billard côtoient un aménagement moderne modéré.

Una arquitectura histórica y una antigua mesa de billar se unen a una decoración moderna discreta.

L'architettura storica e un vecchio tavolo da biliardo si incontrano con un arredamento moderno.

Entering the hotel, one can leisurely check-in in the lobby while enjoying a drink.
Wer das Hotel betritt, kann gemütlich bei einem Drink an der Lobby einchecken.
Celui qui entre dans l'hôtel peut s'inscrire en tout confort au hall devant un drink.
Registrarse cómodamente mientras se disfruta de un trago en el vestíbulo.
Chi entra nell'hotel può disbrigare piacevolmente le formalità davanti a un drink.

The Westin
Sydney, Australia

Located in the center close to the famous Sydney opera, the hotel looks over Martin Place. The guestrooms partially lie in a historically listed old building from 1887, which used to accommodate the post office but also partially lies in a modern tower of 31 floors. The one is distinguished by high ceilings and historic furniture, the other by room-high glazing and a good view. Stores that have settled thanks to the central site of the hotel atrium invite one to go shopping.

Unweit der berühmten Oper von Sydney in der Innenstadt gelegen, schaut das Hotel über Martin Place. Teilweise liegen die Gästezimmer in einem denkmalgeschützten Altbau aus dem Jahr 1887, der früher die Post beherbergte, teilweise aber auch in einem modernen Turm von 31 Stockwerken. Die einen zeichnen sich durch hohe Decken und eine historische Ausstattung aus, die anderen durch raumhohe Verglasungen und eine gute Aussicht. Läden, die dank der zentralen Lage das Atrium des Hotels besiedeln, laden zum Shopping ein.

Situé non loin du célèbre opéra de Sydney dans le centre ville, l'hôtel a vue sur Martin Place. Les chambres des hôtes se trouvent en partie dans un ancien bâtiment datant de 1887 et classé monument historique qui hébergeait autrefois la poste, mais pour une autre partie aussi dans une tour moderne de 31 étages. Les unes se distinguent par des plafonds élevés et un aménagement historique, les autres par des vitrages aussi hauts que la pièce et une belle vue. Les magasins qui occupent l'atrium de l'hôtel grâce à sa position centrale invitent au shopping.

No lejos de la famosa Ópera de Sydney, en el centro de la ciudad, se encuentra el hotel mirando hacia la Martin Place. Las habitaciones están ubicadas, en parte, en una antigua construcción de 1887, declarada patrimonio nacional, que antaño albergara la oficina de correos. Otras se encuentran en una moderna torre de 31 pisos. Las primeras se caracterizan por los techos altos y una decoración histórica, las últimas, por sus altos ventanales y una buena vista. Gracias a su ubicación central, el atrio acoge numerosas tiendas que invitan al shopping.

Situato non lontano dal famoso teatro dell'opera di Sidney nel centro città, l'hotel dà sulla Martin Place. Le camere si trovano in parte in un edificio d'epoca del 1887 sottoposto alla tutela dei beni culturali e un tempo sede della posta, e in parte in una torre moderna di trentun piani. Le prime si distinguono per i soffitti alti e un arredo antico, le altre per le vetrate a tutt'altezza e un bel panorama. I negozi che, grazie alla posizione centrale, colonizzano l'atrio dell'hotel, invitano allo shopping.

Restaurant Mosaic, located in the first upper storey, provides a view of the glass-covered courtyard.

Vom Restaurant Mosaic, das im ersten Obergeschoss liegt, lässt sich der glasüberdachte Hof überblicken.

Du restaurant Mosaic, situé au premier étage, vous pouvez embrasser du regard, la cour recouverte d'un toit en verre.

Desde el restaurante Mosaic, ubicado en el primer piso, se puede mirar hacia el patio con techo de cristal.

Dal ristorante Mosaic, che si trova al primo piano, si vede il cortile sotto la copertura in vetro.

Tradition is rare in Australia, but in the Heritage Wing of the Sydney Westin, it can be sensed in every corner.

Tradition ist selten in Australien, im Heritage Wing des Westin Sydney ist sie jedoch an jeder Ecke zu spüren.

La tradition est rare en Australie, on peut cependant la ressentir à chaque endroit dans le Heritage Wing du Westin Sydney.

Lo tradicional no es muy común en Australia, sin embargo, en el Heritage Wing del Westin Sydney se respira tradición por todas partes.

La tradizione è rara in Australia, ma nell'ala Heritage del Westin di Sidney la si può sentire in ogni angolo.

Hilton Auckland

Auckland, New Zealand

Built on the tip of a wharf, the hotel is surrounded by water on three sides. Each room has a balcony or a terrace with an impressive view of the harbor. At the same time, the Hilton is only a couple of steps from the shopping and business district. Individuality is rated very highly: almost no room is the same as another; each is furnished a bit differently. But common to all is the modern minimalist design and oversized bed.

Auf die Spitze eines Kais gebaut, ist das Hotel auf drei Seiten von Wasser umgeben. Jedes Zimmer hat einen Balkon oder eine Terrasse mit beeindruckender Aussicht über den Hafen. Gleichzeitig ist das Hilton nur ein paar Schritte vom Einkaufs- und Geschäftsviertel entfernt. Individualität wird großgeschrieben: Fast kein Zimmer gleicht dem anderen, jedes ist ein wenig anders eingerichtet. Allen gemeinsam aber ist die moderne minimalistische Gestaltung und das übergroße Bett.

Construit au bout d'un quai, l'hôtel est entouré d'eau sur trois côtés. Chaque chambre a un balcon ou une terrasse avec une vue impressionnante sur le port. De plus, le Hilton ne se trouve qu'à quelques pas du quartier commerçant et du quartier des affaires. L'individualité est écrite en grand : presque aucune chambre ne ressemble à l'autre, chacune est aménagée un peu autrement. Mais toutes ont en commun la réalisation moderne minimaliste et le lit plus grand que la moyenne.

Construido en la punta de un muelle, el hotel está rodeado de agua por tres partes. Cada habitación tiene un balcón o una terraza con vista espectacular del puerto. A la vez, el Hilton está a un paso de la zona comercial y de negocios. La importancia de la individualidad: Casi todas las habitaciones son diferentes, cada una es decorada con algo distinto. Pero todas tienen en común una decoración minimalista y una inmensa cama.

Costruito sulla punta di una banchina, l'hotel è circondato dall'acqua da tre lati. Ogni camera ha un balcone o una terrazza con una sorprendente vista sul porto. Al tempo stesso l'Hilton dista appena due passi dal quartiere commerciale e dei negozi. Individualità con la maiuscola: quasi nessuna camera è uguale all'altra, ognuna è arredata in modo un po' diverso. Comune a tutte, però, è il moderno arredamento minimalistico e l'enorme letto.

Understatement: the reduced, puristic design in the style of classical modernism hardly lets one suspect what luxury is offered the guest.

Understatement: Die reduzierte, puristische Gestaltung im Stil der klassischen Moderne lässt kaum ahnen, welcher Luxus dem Gast geboten wird.

Euphémisme : la réalisation réduite et puriste dans le style de l'art moderne classique laisse à peine deviner le luxe qui est offert à l'hôtel.

Mesura y discreción: El diseño purista y sobrio en el estilo del arte moderno, no deja adivinar el lujo que espera al huésped.

Understatement: l'arredamento essenziale, purista nello stile della modernità classica, non fa presagire al cliente quale lusso gli viene offerto.

In each of the 158 rooms, the guest is greeted by a magnificent panoramic view over the Waitemata Harbor.

In jedem der 158 Zimmer erwartet den Gast ein großartiger Panoramablick über den Waitemata Hafen.

Dans chacune des 158 chambres, une splendide vue panoramique sur le port de Waitemata attend l'hôte.

En cada una de las 158 habitaciones le espera al huésped una vista fantástica del puerto Waitemata.

In ognuna della 158 camere una grandiosa vista panoramica sul Waitemata Harbour attende l'ospite.

The theme of white rules the Hilton inside and out. The building awakens associations of a large ocean liner with its bridge and railing.

Das Thema Weiß beherrscht das Hilton innen wie außen. Das Gebäude weckt Assoziationen an einen großen Ozeandampfer mit seiner Kommandobrücke und seinen Relings.

Le thème du blanc domine le Hilton à l'intérieur comme à l'extérieur. Le bâtiment éveille des associations à un grand bateau à vapeur de l'océan avec sa passerelle de commandement et son bastingage.

El color blanco predomina en el Hilton, tanto en el interior como en el exterior. El edificio nos evoca un buque transatlántico con su puente de mando y la borda.

Il bianco è il tema dominante nell'Hilton, dentro e fuori. L'edificio evoca l'immagine di un grande transatlantico con ponte di comando e parapetti di murata.

Matakauri Lodge

Queenstown, New Zealand

Whoever appreciates silence and a panoramic view of an almost virgin unspoilt mountain range should visit the Matakauri Lodge. Its individual buildings are connected through a lovingly created system of small paths and gardens winding through the terrain above a rocky lakeshore. As all secondary rooms are banned underground, the buildings are especially small and inconspicuous. Wood on ceilings and floor, snow white plastered walls and huge glass surfaces shape the rooms.

Wer Ruhe und einen Panoramablick auf fast jungfräulich unverbaute Bergketten zu schätzen weiß, sollte das Matakauri Lodge besuchen. Seine einzelnen Gebäude sind durch ein liebevoll angelegtes System kleiner Pfade und Gärten verbunden, die sich oberhalb eines felsigen Seeufers durchs Gelände schlängeln. Weil alle Nebenräume unter die Erde verbannt wurden, fallen die Bauten besonders klein und unauffällig aus. Holz an Decke und Boden, schneeweiß verputzte Wände und riesige Glasflächen prägen die Räume.

Qui sait apprécier le calme et une vue panoramique sur des chaînes de montagne presque vierges de constructions devrait descendre au Matakauri Lodge. Ses différents bâtiments sont reliés par un système aménagé avec tendresse de petits sentiers et de jardins qui serpentent à travers le terrain, au-dessus de la rive rocheuse du lac. Etant donné que toutes les pièces secondaires ont été isolées sous terre, les bâtiments donnent une impression particulièrement petite et discrète. Du bois au plafond et au sol, des murs au crépi blanc neige et de gigantesques surfaces en verre caractérisent les pièces.

Aquellos que aprecian la tranquilidad y una vista panorámica de unas cadenas montañosas con escasas construcciones, deberían alojarse en el Matakauri Lodge. Sus construcciones independientes se encuentran unidas a través de un sistema de jardines y pequeños caminos que serpentean por las orillas rocosas del lago, que ha sido diseñado con gran esmero. Ya que todas las habitaciones accesorias han sido condenadas a estar bajo tierra, las construcciones se ven pequeñas y discretas. Madera en los techos y los suelos, paredes enlucidas de blanco y enormes superficies de cristal caracterizan las habitaciones.

Chi sa apprezzare tranquillità e veduta panoramica su catene montuose quasi incontaminate, non deturpate da costruzioni, dovrebbe venire al Matakauri Lodge. I singoli edifici sono collegati da un curatissimo sistema di piccoli sentieri e giardini, che si snodano per tutta l'area al di sopra delle sponde rocciose di un lago. Siccome tutti i ripostigli e le stanze di servizio sono state confinate sotto terra, le costruzioni sono particolarmente piccole e non danno nell'occhio. Soffitti e pavimenti in legno, pareti dall'intonaco candido ed enormi superfici in vetro caratterizzano i locali.

Light floods the bright two-storey suites with their friendly, relatively simple interiors.

Licht durchflutet sind die hellen zweigeschossigen Suiten mit ihrem freundlichen, relativ schlichten Interieur.

Les suites claires et sur deux étages avec leur intérieur agréable et relativement simple sont baignées de lumière.

Las suites dúplex con su acogedor interior, relativamente sobrio, se hallan inundadas de luz.

La luce inonda le suite a due piani con i loro interni accoglienti e relativamente semplici.

The Matakauri Lodge is enthroned above Lake Wakatipu, whose main building, four villas, and a spa pavilion hardly affects the almost untouched countryside.

Über dem Lake Wakatipu thront die Matakauri Lodge, deren Hauptgebäude, vier Villen und ein Spa-Pavillon kaum die fast unberührte Landschaft stören.

Le Matakauri Lodge trône au-dessus du lac Wakatipu, dont le bâtiment principal, quatre villas et un pavillon spa gênent à peine le paysage presque intact.

Sobre el lago Wakatipu se yergue el Matakauri Lodge, cuya edificación principal, cuatro chalés y un pabellón spa apenas alteran el paisaje casi virgen.

Il Matakauri Lodge sovrasta il lago Wakatipu, e i suoi edifici principali, quattro ville e il padiglione delle terme non disturbano il paesaggio quasi intatto.

Index

India

Myanmar

Thailand

Cambodia

Vietnam

Singapore

Indonesia

Bali

Uma Ubud

Jalan Raya Sanggingan, Banjar Lungsiakan, Kedewatan, Ubud, Gianyar 80571, Bali, Indonesia
T +62 (361) 972 448, F +62 (361) 972 449
www.comohotels.co.uk

14 terrace rooms, 10 garden rooms, 3 pool suites, Shambala Suite with infinity pool. Restaurant. Yoga, fitness, sauna. 45 minutes to Denpasar airport.

China

Beijing

The Peninsula Palace Beijing

8 Goldfish Lane, Wangfujing, Beijing 100006, China
T +86 (10) 8516 2888, F +86 (10) 6510 6311
www.peninsula.com

478 rooms and 52 suites. 2 restaurants including Jing restaurant. Bar, lobby lounge. Spa, swimming pool, beauty treatments, meeting facilities. 30 km to the airport.

Shanghai

Grand Hyatt Shanghai

Jin Mao Tower, 88 Century Boulevard, Pudong, Shanghai 200121, China
T +86 (21) 5049 1234, F +86 (21) 5049 1111
www.hyatt.com

555 rooms and suites. A range of restaurants and bars. Indoor pool, spa. Conference facilities for up to 1.200 people. Located on the 53rd to 87th floors of the Jin Mao Tower. 30 minutes to the airport.

Hong Kong

Hong Kong

The Peninsula

Salisbury Road, Kowloon, Hong Kong
T +852 2920 2888, F +852 2722 4170
www.peninsula.com

244 rooms, 54 suites. 7 restaurants including Felix restaurant, bar. Spa, health club. Meeting facilities. Helicopter transfers. Located at the heart of Kowloon, 40 minutes to the airport.

Hong Kong

Grand Hyatt Plateau

1 Harbour Road, Hong Kong
T +852 2588 1234, F +852 2802 0677
www.hyatt.com

556 rooms and suites. 6 restaurants, bar. Convention facilities. Outdoor swimming pool, fitness studios. Located on the waterfront, 5 minutes to the shopping district, 40 km to the airport.

Hong Kong

Mandarin Oriental

5 Connaught Road, Central Hong Kong
T +852 2522 0111, F +852 2810 6190
www.mandarinoriental.com

486 rooms, 55 suites. 4 restaurants, lounge, 2 bars, cake shop. Indoor swimming pool, fitness room. Conference facilities for up to 600 people. 45 minutes to the airport.

Hong Kong

Le Meridien Cyberport

100, Cyberport Road, Hong Kong
T +852 2980 7788, F +852 2980 7888
www.lemeridien.com

173 rooms and suites. Club floors. 2 restaurants, 2 lounges, bar. Conference facilities. Outdoor pool, fitness. 15 minutes to business district, 40 minutes to the airport.

Taiwan

Taipei

Les Suites Taipei

12 Ching Cheng Street, Taipei 105, Taiwan
T +886 (2) 8712 7688, F +886 (2) 8712 7699
www.suitetpe.com.tw

90 rooms including 16 suites. 1 VIP Suite. Lounge and bar for breakfast. Complimentary snacks and drinks from 6 am till midnight. Small garden. Situated in downtown Taipei, 10 minutes to the airport.

Sun Moon Lake

The Lalu

142 Jungshing Road, Yuchr Shiang Nantou, Taiwan
T +886 (049) 285 5311, F +886 (049) 285 5312
www.ghmhotels.com

96 rooms, suites and villas. 4 restaurants, bar and lounge. Spa, tennis, swimming pool. Located at the Sun Moon Lake, 1,5 hours to Taichung Airport, 3,5 hours to the airport.

Japan

Mochi

Mojiko Hotel

9-11 Minato-machi, Moji-ku, Kitakyushu, Fukuoka, Japan
T +81 (93) 321 1111, F +81 (93) 321 7111
www.mojiko-hotel.com

134 rooms. 3 restaurants. Meeting facilities. Located in the heart of Mojiko Retro area.

Nasu Gun

Niki Club

2301 Takakuotsu, Michishita, Nasu-machi, Nasu-gun, Tochigi-ken 3250303 Japan
T +81 (287) 78 2215, F +81 (287) 78 2218
www.nikiclub.jp

42 rooms. Restaurant and bar. Spa, tennis. Meeting room for up to 35 people. Located in Nasu, 2 hours drive from Tokyo.

Tokyo

Park Hyatt Tokyo

3-7-1-2 Nishi-Shinjuku, Shinjuku-ku, Tokyo, Japan 163-1055
T +81 (3) 5322 1234, F +81 (3) 5322 1288
www.tokyo.park.hyatt.com

155 rooms, 22 suites, presidential suite. 4 restaurants, 2 bars, lounge. Health and fitness sanctuary. Business center, conference facilities.

Tokyo

Four Seasons Hotel Tokyo at Marunouchi

Pacific Century Place, 1-11-1 Marunouchi, Chiyoda-ku, Tokyo, Japan 100 6277
T +81 (3) 5222 7222, F +81 (3) 5222 1255
www.fourseasons.com

57 rooms including 9 suites. Restaurant, private dining rooms. Health club, spa. Business center.

Tokyo

The Strings Hotel

Shinagawa East One Tower, 2-16-1 Konan, Minato-ku, Tokyo, Japan 108 8282
T +81 (3) 4562 1111, F +81 (3) 4562 1112
www.stringshotel.com

200 rooms. Restaurant and bar. Located in the heart of Metropolitan Tokyo.

Australia

Melbourne

Hotel Lindrum

26 Flinders Street, Melbourne, Victoria 3000, Australia
T +61 (3) 9668 1111, F +61 (3) 9668 1199
www.hotellindrum.com.au

59 rooms. Restaurant, lobby, cigar bar, lounge. Health club. Meeting facilities for small meetings. Located in the heart of Melbourne.

Sydney

The Westin

1 Martin Place, Sydney, New South Wales 2000, Australia
T +61 (2) 8223 1111, F +61 (2) 8223 1222
www.westin.com

416 rooms within 2 distinctive buildings. 2 restaurants, bar, lobby lounge. Conference facilities for up to 1.200 guests.

New Zealand

Auckland

Hilton Auckland

Princess Wharf, 147 Quay Street, Auckland, New Zealand
T +64 (9) 978 2000, F +64 (9) 978 2001
www.hilton.com

233 rooms and suites. 4 bars, restaurant. Swimming pool, gym. Meeting facilities for up to 460 people. Located on the waterfront.

Queenstown

Matakauri Lodge

Glenorchy Road, PO Box 888, Queenstown, New Zealand
T +64 (3) 441 1008, F +64 (3) 441 2180
www.matakauri.co.nz

4 villas and 3 suites. Dining room with fireplace. Wine cellar. Spa, gym. A 10 minutes drive to Queenstown.

Photo Credits

Editor Martin Nicholas Kunz

Editorial coordination Patricia Massó

Introduction Camilla Péus

Hotel texts by Camilla Péus
Christian Schönwetter
Martin Nicholas Kunz

Layout & Prepress Käthe Nennstiel

Imaging Susanne Olbrich

Translations
English: Robert Kaplan, Ade Team
French: Celine Verschelde, SAW Communications
Spanish: Cristina Franco
Italian: Evita Santopietro, SAW Communications

Editorial project by fusion publishing gmbh, Berlin
www.fusion-publishing.com

Published by teNeues Publishing Group

teNeues Verlag GmbH + Co.KG
Am Selder 37, 47906 Kempen, Germany
Tel.: 0049-(0)2152-916-0, Fax: 0049-(0)2152-916-111
Press department: arehn@teneues.de

teNeues Publishing Company
16 West 22nd Street, New York, NY 10010, US
Tel.: 001-212-627-9090, Fax: 001-212-627-9511

teNeues Publishing UK Ltd.
York Villa, York Road
Byfleet
KT14 7HX, Great Britain
Tel.: 0044-1932-403509, Fax: 0044-1932-403514

teNeues France S.A.R.L.
93 rue Bannier
4500 Orléans, France
Tel.: 0033-2-38541071, Fax: 0033-1-38625340

www.teneues.com

©2009 teNeues Verlag GmbH + Co. KG, Kempen

Anniversary Edition

ISBN: 978-3-8327-9332-6

Printed in Italy